WOMAN'S OWN

CHRISTMAS COOKING

CHRISTMAS COOKING

Woman's Own Cookery Collection

GINA STEER
COOKERY CONSULTANT FOR WOMAN'S OWN

NOTES

Both metric and imperial measurements have been used in all recipes.
Use one set of measurements only and not a mixture of both.

Standard level spoon measurements are used in all recipes
1 tablespoon = one 15 ml spoon
1 teaspoon = one 5 ml spoon

Ovens should be preheated to the specific temperature.
If using a fan assisted oven, follow manufacturer's instructions
for adjusting the temperature.

First published 1992
Hamlyn is an imprint of
Octopus Illustrated Publishing,
part of Reed International Books Limited,
Michelin House, 81 Fulham Road,
London, SW3 6RB

A catalogue record for this book is available from the British Library

ISBN 0 600 57622 1

Produced by Mandarin Offset
Printed and Bound in Hong Kong

CONTENTS

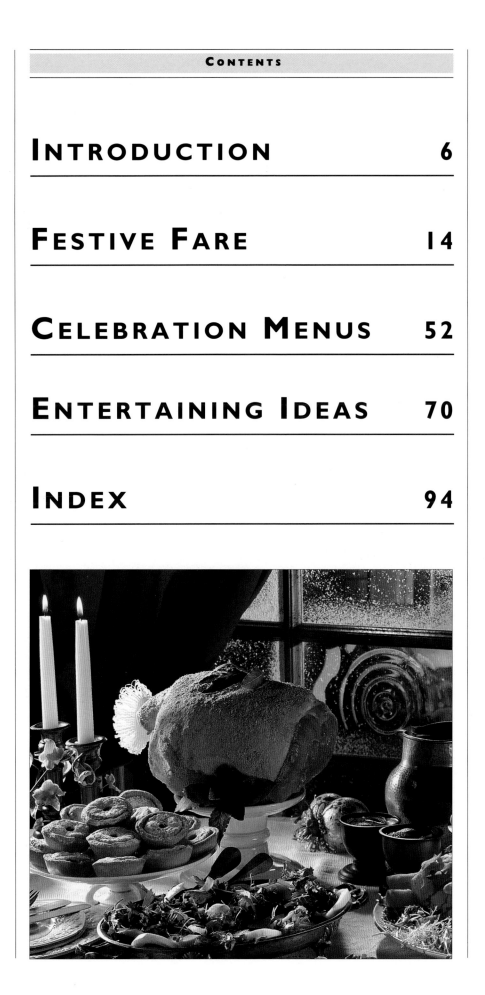

Christmas is a time for giving and receiving, for laughter and gaiety, but also for eating and drinking. It features perhaps the most enjoyable meal of the year…the Christmas feast.

Most of us love the traditional roast turkey with all the trimmings, the cranberry and bread sauce, crunchy roast potatoes and parsnips, buttery sprouts and chestnuts followed by Christmas pudding with brandy butter, sherry trifle or chocolate roulade, nuts, dates, home-made truffles, mince pies and Christmas cake.

However it doesn't stop at the Christmas meal. There's also the rest of the festive season to think about including Christmas Eve, Boxing Day and the days leading up to and including New Year's Day. All this needs catering for, and that's where this Christmas book will ease the panic from your life. It provides a host of recipes and ideas to help you sail through the festive season with a smile on your face and still enables you to enjoy yourself with your family and friends.

This book is designed to help you plan ahead with a variety of different ideas, menus, including vegetarian alternatives, and recipes from all over the world.

All the recipes have been developed and tested in the Woman's Own test kitchen, you can cook them with confidence knowing that they will work and that you'll be able to give everyone a Christmas to remember. So get planning and cooking and you'll enjoy the best Christmas ever.

Happy Christmas

Gina Steer

Gina Steer

PLAN AHEAD

Planning the festive meals in advance makes the countdown to Christmas so much easier and enables you to relax and not worry; you'll know you have everything completely under control.

3 MONTHS AHEAD:

- Make Christmas Pudding, replace greaseproof paper, tin foil or pudding-cloth then store in a cool, dry, dark place.
- Make Christmas Cake, leave in tin until completely cold then remove and leave lining paper intact. Prick the top with a skewer then drizzle over about 2 tbsp of brandy. Wrap in greaseproof paper and tin foil or brown paper and store in a cool dry place. Repeat drizzling with the brandy 2 or 3 times more in the next 2 months.

2 MONTHS AHEAD:

- Plan menus for the festive season.
- Order turkey, sausages and any other meat and fish that will be required.
- Make shopping lists for groceries and start buying to spread the cost.
- Make mincemeat if using home-made, allow to mature.
- Buy or order Christmas cards, check out overseas posting dates. Plan Christmas present ideas, start buying wherever possible.

1 MONTH AHEAD:

- Make and freeze mince pies, (after thawing warm through before serving).
- Make any alternative dishes, such as terrines, pies, desserts and bakes if suitable for freezing, freeze then wrap and label clearly.
- Write Christmas cards, buy stamps ready for posting. Check posting dates.
- Check Christmas tree decorations, decide on table and room decorations.

3 WEEKS AHEAD:

- Check Christmas Cake, give a final drizzle of brandy.
- Check menus and make final shopping lists.
- Order milk and cream from milkman.
- Buy gift wrap and tags, start wrapping.
- Check crockery, glasses and cutlery.
- Check wines, liqueurs and soft drinks.
- Order any fresh flowers, holly or mistletoe.

2 WEEKS AHEAD:

- Make almond paste for Christmas Cake and apply.
- Make and freeze brandy butter.
- Do any extra jobs such as cleaning silver, windows etc. Check with your butcher when you can collect your fresh turkey and other meats.

A traditional round Christmas Pudding

I WEEK AHEAD:

• Decorate Christmas Cake, leave lightly covered to protect from dust.
• Do remainder of grocery shopping, leaving the perishables until last. If possible order your greengrocery.
• Make truffles if serving home-made ones, store wrapped in fridge.
• Make and freeze breadcrumbs ready for stuffing and bread sauce.
• Buy Christmas tree if using a fresh one, and decorate.
• Check times of Church services for the festive season.

3-4 DAYS BEFORE:

• Check defrosting times for frozen turkey, leave in fridge to defrost.
• Collect fresh turkey, sausages and other meats ordered from butcher.
• Prepare rooms for any overnight guests.

CHRISTMAS EVE:

• Defrost breadcrumbs for stuffing and bread sauce.
• Prepare turkey for cooking, stuff the neck flap, wrap in foil, leave in fridge.
• Prepare bacon rolls, sausagemeat balls, if making, prepare giblet stock for gravy, leave all covered in fridge.
• Soak ham if cooking a gammon joint.
• Prepare potatoes and parsnips and any other root vegetables, leave covered with cold water. Prepare carrots, sprouts and salad ingredients, leave in polythene bags in fridge.
• Prepare cranberry sauce if using fresh cranberries.
• Prepare starters if necessary, cover and leave in fridge.
• Defrost mince pies and any other desserts if frozen.

HINTS AND TIPS FOR BUYING AND COOKING TURKEY

- When buying frozen turkey, avoid any with damaged packaging or any that contains pinkish ice (which means that the bird has been partially thawed and then refrozen).
- If possible, use a cool bag with freezer blocks for carrying the frozen bird home after purchase. Place in freezer immediately you get home.
- Cook a fresh turkey within 2 days of purchase. Keep loosely covered in fridge. Rinse well before using.
- Never, ever refreeze thawed turkey unless it has been thoroughly cooked first.
- If using a frozen turkey always ensure that it is thoroughly defrosted before cooking. Leave the turkey in its polythene bag to defrost and if possible defrost in a fridge, never in a warm room. (You can defrost in

A delicious roast turkey for Christmas Day

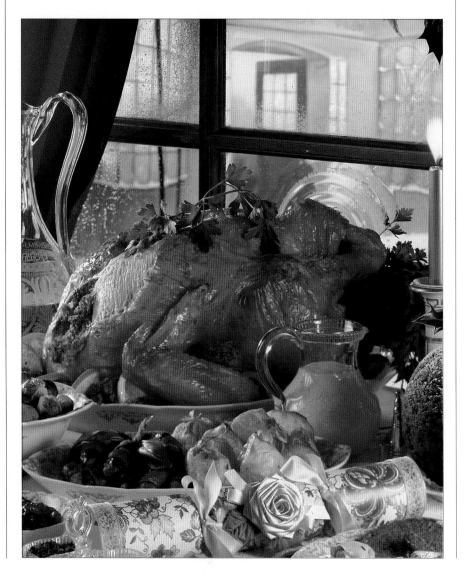

cold water to speed up the defrosting process, but you must change the water frequently.)
- After defrosting the turkey, keep in the fridge and cook within 1 day.
- Once completely defrosted, remove the giblets, if there are any, rinse the bird thoroughly under cold running water, inside and out, and pat dry.
- When preparing turkey, use a clean board and implements, and wipe everything down with disinfectant. Wash hands afterwards.
- It is no longer recommended that you stuff the cavity of the bird, in case any bacteria present is not completely killed during the cooking process.
- After cooking do not freeze the meat on the carcass. Cut off the meat and freeze (to avoid the meat drying out, place in stock or gravy before freezing). Freeze stuffing separately.

DEFROSTING GUIDE FOR FROZEN TURKEY

A 5-8 lb/2.25-3 kg turkey will take 2-2½ hrs in the fridge
  (15-18 hours in cold water)

An 8-12 lb/3.5-5.5 kg turkey takes 2½ -3 days in the fridge
  (18-24 hours in cold water).

A 12-14 lb/5.5-6.5 kg turkey takes 3-3½ days in the fridge,
  (24-26 hours in cold water.)

QUANTITY GUIDE

A 5-8 lb/2.25-3 kg turkey will serve 6-10 people

An 8-12 lb/3.5-5 kg turkey will serve 12-16 people

A 12-14 lb/5.5-6.5 kg turkey will serve 16-20 people

If using a frozen turkey you must ensure that it is thoroughly defrosted before cooking.

ROASTING CHART

Size of Bird	Cooking Times	Temperature
8-12 lb/3.5-5.5 kg	25 mins per lb + 20 mins	Gas 4 350°F/180°C
12-15 lb/5.5-7 kg	20 mins per lb + 20 mins	Gas 4 350°F/180°C
15-20 lb/7-9 kg	18 mins per lb + 18 mins	Gas 4 350°F/180°C

EASY PARTY IDEAS

Make it possible to throw a party and have time to enjoy the food and relax with your guests. With careful planning and the right menu you can serve delicious imaginative food using any leftovers from Christmas Day.

• Choose food that is varied in appearance, colour and texture.
• Make dishes that can be prepared in advance, cold food that doesn't go soggy and hot food that is quick to reheat.
• If the party is a stand-up affair, make sure guests can easily pick up the food from the serving platter and eat it in one bite.
• Use seasonal ingredients and avoid very complicated or extravagant dishes when entertaining a larger number of guests.
• Sausage rolls, canapés and quiche are quick and easy, simply oven bake straight from the freezer.
• Don't waste money on classic wines - serve punch as it is more versatile and lasts longer.
• Easy dips can be made at the last minute by mixing curry powder, mustard and cream cheese into a thick mayonnaise.
• Provide a selection of fruit juices, mineral water, low alcohol beer and wine for the drivers.

A selection of tasty canapé ideas (see pages 48-49 for recipes)

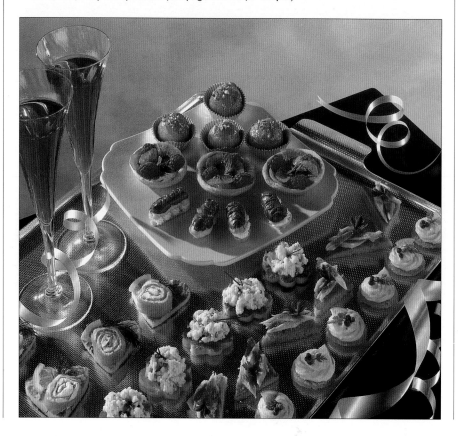

CHRISTMAS DAY TIMEPLAN

9.30 am   Time for a leisurely breakfast, opening presents and organizing the family.

10.00 am   Put prepared turkey (10 lb/4.5 kg) in oven, parboil potatoes and parsnips, infuse milk for bread sauce. Cut sprig of holly for Christmas Pudding. Decorate any additional dessert if not already done.
Get family to clear away breakfast and, lay the table for Christmas lunch. Tidy up wrapping paper etc.

11.15 am   Check and baste turkey. Chill white wine, if using. Prepare and garnish starters if having, leave lightly covered in a cool place. Make bread sauce, cover lightly.

12.00 pm   Put home-made Christmas Pudding on to steam, or follow manufacturer's instructions

1.30 pm   Increase oven temperature, then place potatoes and parsnips in oven to roast. Open red wine and allow to breathe. Check water in steamer for Christmas Pudding.

1.45 pm   Turn back foil from turkey, baste. Cook sausages, bacon rolls, baste potatoes and parsnips. Take brandy butter out of fridge to soften. Place mince pies on baking sheet to warm through once turkey is cooked and oven switched off.

2.00 pm   Cook remaining vegetables. Remove turkey and allow to rest for 15 mins before carving. Make gravy.

2.15 pm   Dish up vegetables, garnish turkey with all the trimmings, serve bread sauce, cranberry sauce and gravy. Turn Christmas Pudding out onto plate, cover lightly and keep warm. Place brandy in a small saucepan to flame the Christmas Pudding (don't warm through until ready to serve).

2.30 pm   Have the best Christmas lunch ever, but don't forget the Queen's speech at 3 pm.

Happy cooking

DELICIOUS IDEAS WITH POULTRY

Chicken and turkey are both popular, because they are versatile and delicious. They are both extremely healthy as they are low in saturated fat, even more so if you discard the skin. These mouthwatering dishes are ideal for any occasion; you and your family will love them.

SPANISH CHICKEN CASSEROLE

4 chicken quarters
3 tbsp olive oil
I Spanish onion, peeled and sliced
I-2 garlic cloves, peeled and finely
  chopped
I red pepper, deseeded and sliced
I orange pepper, deseeded and sliced
I green pepper, deseeded and sliced
¼ pint/I50 ml chicken stock
few saffron strands
¼ pint/I50 ml dry white wine
salt and freshly ground black pepper
I tbsp cornflour
flat leaf parsley sprig to garnish

SERVES 4 • CALORIES PER PORTION: 322

Preheat the oven to Gas 4, 350°F, 180°C. Wash and dry the chicken quarters. Remove the skin, if preferred. Heat 2 tbsp oil in a frying pan. Fry the chicken quarters on all sides until sealed ,and golden then drain on a piece of kitchen paper and place in a 4 pint/2.25 litre casserole.

Add the remaining oil to the frying pan, then fry the onion, garlic and peppers for 5 mins, or until softened. Using a slotted spoon, drain the vegetables and garlic and add to casserole.

In the cleaned frying pan, heat the chicken stock with the saffron strands, leave to infuse for 5 mins, then strain and pour over the chicken quarters. Add the dry white wine. Season with salt and freshly ground black pepper, mix lightly together then cover the casserole and cook in the oven for I hr, or until the chicken is completely cooked.

Drain off the liquid to a clean, small pan and heat to boiling point. Blend the cornflour with 3 tbsp water, then stir it into the liquid. Cook, stirring throughout, until the sauce has thickened. Pour over the contents of the casserole and serve immediately, garnished with flat leaf parsley.

STUFFED DUCK LEGS WITH PLUM SAUCE

This recipe works equally well if
chicken legs are used instead of
the duck.

2 duck legs
salt and freshly ground black pepper
FOR THE STUFFING:
2 spring onions, trimmed and
  chopped
2 oz/50 g long-grain rice, cooked
grated rind of ½ lemon
2 tbsp water chestnuts, chopped
2 ripe plums, stoned and chopped
I oz/25 g fresh white breadcrumbs
I egg, size 5, beaten
FOR THE PLUM SAUCE:
2 plums, stoned and chopped
I tbsp clear honey
2 tsp wine vinegar
I tsp arrowroot
dill sprigs to garnish

SERVES 2 • CALORIES PER PORTION: 581

Preheat the oven to Gas 4, 350°F, 180°C. Bone the duck legs, as described on the following pages, wash and dry the meat, then season with salt and freshly ground black pepper. Mix together the spring onions, cooked rice, lemon rind, water chestnuts, plums and breadcrumbs. Add the egg, then mix together. Divide the stuffing between duck legs, fold over to encase stuffing and secure each, as described on the following pages.

Place duck legs in a roasting tin and cook for 30 mins, or until cooked. Remove from the oven, discard string and cover with foil to keep warm.

To make the sauce, place the plums, honey and vinegar in a small pan with ¼ pint/I50 ml water. Heat through. Blend the arrowroot with I tbsp water, then stir into the pan. Bring to the boil then cook, stirring throughout, until the sauce thick-

Clockwise from bottom left: Turkey Roulade, Spanish Chicken Casserole, Warm Duck Salad, Roast Turkey with Orange & Hazelnut Stuffing, Roast Duck with Cherry Sauce, Stuffed Duck Legs with Plum Sauce

ROAST DUCK WITH CHERRY SAUCE

I oven-ready duck, approx 4 lb/1.75 kg in weight
I small cooking apple, washed and quartered
I small onion, peeled and quartered
FOR THE SAUCE:
½ pint/300 ml chicken or vegetable stock
I tbsp clear honey
I tbsp light soy sauce
3 oz/75 g red cherries, pitted and roughly chopped
I fresh fig, wiped and roughly chopped
cherries, sliced fresh figs and parsley to garnish

SERVES 4 • CALORIES PER PORTION: 247

Preheat the oven to Gas 4, 350°F, 180°C. Weigh the duck and calculate cooking time (see chart opposite). Prepare and roast the duck, as described in the tip, placing the quartered cooking apple and quartered onion inside the cavity. Roast the duck for the calculated cooking time.

To make the cherry sauce, heat together the chicken or vegetable stock, honey and soy sauce until the honey has dissolved, then boil rapidly until reduced by half. Add the cherries and the chopped fig to the pan, then cook for 2 mins. Pour into a sauce boat and serve with the roast duck, garnished with cherries, sliced fresh figs and parsley sprigs.

---

ens and clears. Serve the sauce with the stuffed duck legs, freshly cooked vegetables and savoury rice. Garnish with dill sprigs.

WARM DUCK SALAD

2 boned duck breasts, each weighing approx 6 oz/175 g
salad leaves, washed
3 oz/75 g shelled pecan nuts
4 oz/100 g yellow cherry tomatoes
I small onion, peeled and sliced into rings
FOR THE DRESSING:
I tbsp clear honey
I tbsp Hoisin sauce
3 tbsp olive oil

SERVES 4 • CALORIES PER PORTION: 387

Preheat grill to high. Wash and dry the duck breasts, then place on rack and grill both sides for 3 mins or until sealed. Reduce heat, then continue to grill for 10-12 mins, or until cooked. Drain on kitchen paper. Arrange the salad leaves in a bowl with the pecan nuts, cherry tomatoes and onion. Place the dressing ingredients in a small pan and heat through, stirring frequently.

Cut the cooked breast into bite-sized pieces and arrange over salad. Pour the warm dressing over and serve immediately.

HANDY TIPS

To roast a duck: discard any fat from the inside of the duck, then rinse and dry thoroughly. Place a peeled and quartered cooking apple and onion inside the cavity, then place bird on a trivet which allows the duck to stand at least 2 in/5 cm proud of the roasting tin. Prick the duck all over with a fork (this enables the fat to run out of the duck, collect in the roasting tin and be discarded). Baste during cooking with its own juices, as this helps to extract fat.

TURKEY ROULADE

1 boneless turkey breast, skinned,
   approx 3 lb/1.5 kg in weight
salt and freshly ground black pepper
FOR THE STUFFING:
1 oz/25 g butter or margarine
1 small onion, peeled and chopped
1 small cooking apple, chopped
3 oz/75 g button mushrooms, wiped
   and chopped
grated rind and juice of 1 lime
3 oz/75 g fresh white breadcrumbs
1 oz/25 g pine kernels
2 tbsp freshly chopped parsley
1 egg, size 3, beaten
1 tbsp clear honey
2 tsp soy sauce
apple slices and mint sprigs to
   garnish

SERVES 4 • CALORIES PER PORTION: 663

Preheat the oven to Gas 4, 350°F, 180°C. Place the turkey breast between two sheets of clearwrap then, skinned side up, beat with a meat mallet until flattened. Start at one end and proceed down the length and width. Wash and dry the turkey breast, then season.

To make the stuffing, melt the fat in a large saucepan. Add the onion and apple, then sauté for 3 mins. Add the mushrooms and continue cooking for a further 3 mins. Remove from the heat and stir in the lime rind and juice, fresh breadcrumbs, pine kernels and chopped parsley. Season to taste. Add the beaten egg and mix to a stiff consistency.

Spoon the stuffing over the prepared turkey breast, to within ½ in/1.25 cm of the edge, then roll up tightly and secure at 2 in/5 cm intervals.

Place meat in a roasting tin. Mix the honey and soy sauce together and use to brush over the roulade. Reserve the remaining honey mixture.

Cover the roulade with tin foil and cook in preheated oven for 1½ hrs, or until the meat is completely cooked. During the last 30 mins of the cooking time, remove the tin foil and brush the turkey with more honey and soy sauce. Repeat at least twice more before the roulade is cooked.

Remove from the oven, discard the string and cut the roulade into 1 in/2.5 cm slices. Arrange on a plate, then serve hot or cold, garnished with apple slices and mint sprigs.

ROAST TURKEY WITH ORANGE & HAZELNUT STUFFING

1 dressed turkey, approx 8 lb/3.5 kg
   in weight
1½ oz/40 g butter, softened, or low-
   fat spread
grated rind of 1 small orange
salt and freshly ground black pepper
bunch of fresh herbs
FOR THE STUFFING BALLS:
1 in/2.5 cm root ginger, peeled
3 oz/75 g hazelnuts, finely chopped
4 spring onions, trimmed and finely
   chopped
grated rind of 1 small orange
4 oz/100 g breadcrumbs
1 egg, size 5, beaten
2 tsp olive oil
tarragon sprigs and satsuma
   segments to garnish

SERVES 8 • CALORIES PER PORTION: 559

Preheat the oven to Gas 4, 350°F, 180°C. Wash and dry turkey, calculate the cooking time (see the chart opposite). Beat together the fat and orange rind. Spread mixture under skin, to flavour the meat.

Season cavity of the turkey, place the fresh herbs inside. Truss, as described on this page, then place in a roasting tin and cover lightly with tin foil. Roast for the calculated cooking time, removing the foil for the last 30 mins. Prepare stuffing balls. Finely grate ginger, place in a bowl with 1 oz/25 g of the hazelnuts. Add spring onions, orange rind, breadcrumbs and seasoning to taste. Add egg, then mix to a stiff, but not sticky, consistency. Shape into small balls, roll in the remaining hazelnuts. Brush lightly with oil, then place in a small roasting tin and cook for the last 30 mins of turkey cooking time.

Serve the stuffing balls with the roast turkey. Garnish.

STUFFING & COOKING A TURKEY

Ensure turkey is completely thawed before stuffing. Wash and dry the bird thoroughly, both inside and out. Prepare stuffing and use in the neck cavity only, secure neck flap. If liked, place a whole lemon and fresh herbs inside cavity. Calculate cooking time then roast the turkey in a preheated oven. To ensure the bird is cooked through, insert a skewer in the thickest part of the thigh, if the juices run clear it is cooked.

CARVING A TURKEY

Once the turkey is cooked, allow to stand for 30 mins then remove from roasting tin and place on serving platter. Using a sharp knife cut off the drumstick at thigh joint . When carving the thigh meat, slice around the leg joint, cutting down towards the parson's nose. Lift the wing away from the turkey and cut off. Carve the breast meat in even slices, starting at the cavity end and moving along towards the stuffing. When carving the drumstick, follow the line of the bone. You may find this easier to do if you hold the tip of the drumstick with a piece of kitchen paper. Arrange the carved meat on a warm platter and if necessary, cover loosely with foil and keep warm. When serving, place slices of dark and white meat on each plate.

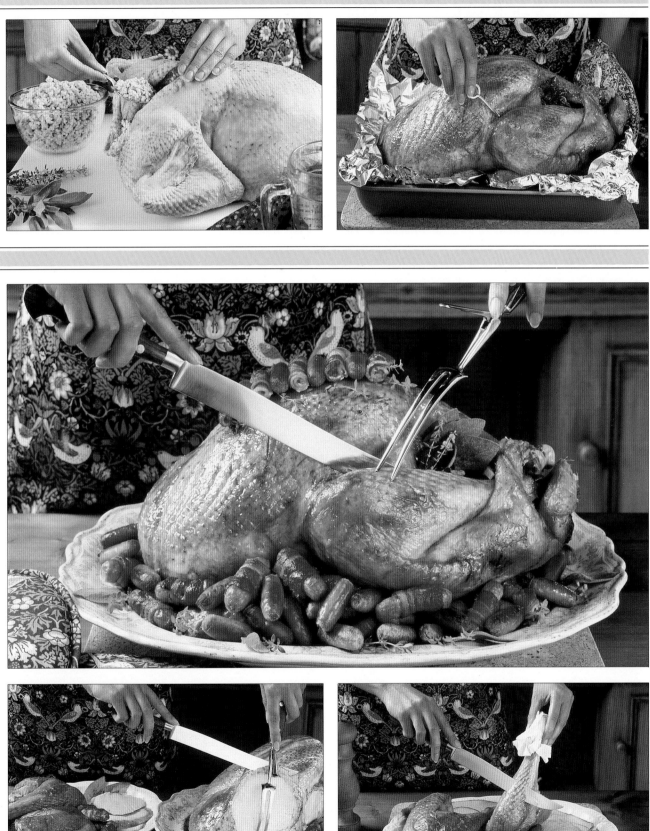

CHRISTMAS CAKE IDEAS

Surprise your family and bake them each a special Christmas cake! We show you how with four super, festive recipes that can be made well in advance then decorated just before the festive season!

BASIC CHRISTMAS CAKE RECIPE

Use this basic Christmas Cake Recipe when making the Snowflake Cake or Christmas Wreath.

8 oz/225 g plain flour
8 oz/225 g butter or margarine
8 oz/225 g soft light brown sugar
4 eggs, size 3, beaten
½ tsp nutmeg
½ tsp mixed spice
8 oz/225 g currants
12 oz/350 g sultanas
8 oz/225 g no-need-to-soak dried
    peaches, chopped
4 oz/100 g hazelnuts, finely chopped
8 tsp brandy or rum
grated rind and juice of 1 orange

MAKES 8 IN/20.5 CM CAKE
CALORIES PER SLICE: 250

Sieve flour into a mixing bowl. In a separate large mixing bowl, cream the fat and sugar until light and fluffy. Gradually add the eggs and beat well. If mixture begins to curdle, add a little flour. Fold in flour and spices, then stir in remaining ingredients. Mix well.

Spoon mixture into prepared tin. Level top, then make a small hollow in the centre to allow for rising. Bake for specified time.

Leave overnight to cool in the tin, then turn out and remove greaseproof paper. Wrap cake in clean greaseproof and store in a dark place for 3 weeks, or until required. When the paper becomes sticky, the cake has matured and can be covered with marzipan.

Always trim the top and turn the cake upside down to ensure a smooth surface before brushing with apricot glaze then covering with marzipan.

SNOWFLAKE CAKE

1 x prepared Basic Christmas Cake
    Recipe mixture
1 lb/450 g white marzipan
3 tbsp apricot jam, sieved
2 lb/900 g royal icing mix
gold food colouring powder
candles to decorate

CUTS INTO 30 SLICES
CALORIES PER SLICE: 378

Preheat the oven to Gas 1, 275°F, 140°C. Grease an 8 in/20.5 cm round cake tin, then line with a double layer of greaseproof paper. Spoon cake mixture into tin, then bake for 4-4½ hrs, or until a skewer inserted in centre comes out clean. Store as described in Basic Christmas Cake Recipe. Drizzle with brandy, if liked.

Remove the greaseproof paper and, if necessary, trim surface of the cake until flat. Measure depth of cake and, on a surface dusted with icing sugar, roll out two-thirds of marzipan to go around side. Roll out remaining marzipan to fit the top of the cake.

Heat jam in a bowl over a pan of hot water, stir then use to brush over sides and top of cake. Place the long strip of marzipan around side of cake and trim to fit. Place the top piece of marzipan on the cake and join edges, pressing with a round-bladed knife. Wrap cake loosely in greaseproof paper and store for 2-3 days to allow the marzipan to dry out thoroughly.

When ready to ice, transfer the cake to an icing turntable. Following instructions, make up 1½ lb/675 g royal icing. Using a palette knife, carefully spread two-thirds of icing around sides of cake. Reserve remaining third, keep covered. Holding edge of knife against icing on cake, rotate turntable with the other hand to smooth

icing. Repeat until sides are completely smooth. Remove any excess icing from around the top edge of the cake.

Place reserved icing on top of cake and, using a palette knife and a paddling motion, smooth top, then move knife backwards and forwards until icing is completely flat. Leave to dry. Once dry, coating may be repeated if necessary. Transfer cake to a 9 in/23 cm round cake board.

Next, trace at least 45 snowflake shapes on to baking parchment. Make up remaining icing, and place two-thirds in a piping bag fitted with a No 2 plain nozzle. Reserve remaining third, keeping it

covered. Turn over parchment and pipe snowflakes on to paper, following the lines showing through. Leave to set for 24 hrs.

Place the reserved icing in a piping bag fitted with a No 2 star nozzle and pipe a shell design around the top and base of the cake. Leave to set.

Carefully remove all the snowflakes from the parchment paper and, using any remaining royal icing, attach the snowflakes around the sides and on top of the cake. Mix a little gold food colouring with a few drops of water and, using a clean paint brush, carefully paint the snowflakes as liked. Leave cake to dry completely.

Secure candles on to the cake with a little icing and leave to set.

Clockwise from top left: Snowflake Cake, Christmas Wreath Cake and 'Small Cake' (bottom left), Vegetarian Fruit & Nut-topped Cake (see page 20)

CHRISTMAS WREATH & 'SMALL CAKE'

1 x prepared Basic Christmas Cake Recipe mixture
1 lb 5 oz/575 g white marzipan
6 tbsp apricot jam, sieved
3 lb/1.5 kg ready-to-roll fondant icing
yellow food colouring
dark brown food colouring powder
light green food colouring powder
dark green food colouring powder
red food colouring

CUTS INTO 34 SLICES
CALORIES PER SLICE: 529

Preheat the oven to Gas 1, 275°F, 140°C. Grease an 8 in/20.5 cm round cake tin, then line with a double layer of greaseproof paper. Spoon the prepared cake mixture into the tin, then bake for 4-4½ hrs, or until a skewer inserted in the centre comes out clean. Store as

described in the Basic Christmas Cake Recipe.

Remove the greaseproof and, if necessary, trim surface of the cake until flat. Cut out and reserve a 4 in/10 cm circle from the centre of cake to use for small Christmas cake.

On a surface dusted with icing sugar, roll out 1 lb/450 g marzipan to a 13 in/33 cm circle. Heat jam in a bowl over a pan of hot water, then brush over wreath-shaped cake, reserving any remaining jam. Place the marzipan over, then cut a cross in centre so that it also covers inner edge of cake. Trim excess marzipan. Wrap cake loosely in greaseproof paper and store for 2-3 days to dry out the marzipan.

On a surface dusted with icing sugar, roll out 5 oz/150 g marzipan to fit over small cake. Coat small cake with reserved jam, then cover with marzipan, as described in the Snowflake Cake recipe. Wrap and store as before. Place wreath on a 10 in/25.5 cm cake board and small cake on a 5 in/12.5 cm cake board.

To ice the wreath, roll out 1 lb/450 g icing into a 14 in/36 cm circle, then use to cover cake, using same technique as for marzipan.

To ice the small cake, roll out 6 oz/175 g icing into a 9 in/23 cm circle and mould over cake to cover completely.

Next, make Christmas roses for wreath cake. On a surface dusted with icing sugar, roll out 3 oz/75 g icing until ¼ in/6 mm thick. Cut 25 petal shapes from icing and, using a cocktail stick, gently roll until paper thin. Line 5 compartments of an egg box with cones of baking parchment, then position 5 petals in each cone, overlapping them to form a rose shape. Colour ½ oz/15 g icing with a little yellow food colouring, then form into 5 small balls. Press a ball into the centre of each rose. Leave to dry overnight.

Roll out remaining fondant and using holly and ivy leaf cutters, cut out about 225 leaves. In 3 separate bowls, mix small amounts of brown and both green food colourings with a little water and, using a paint brush, paint leaves. Leave to dry.

Using the light green food colouring, carefully paint the icing covering the cake.

Colour the offcuts of icing from the leaves with red food colouring and roll into small balls for the holly berries.

Brush cake with water and reserving a few leaves and berries for small cake, arrange remaining leaves and berries on wreath cake. Remove roses from egg box and secure on wreath cake.

Arrange reserved leaves and berries on top of small cake and attach a ribbon around middle.

VEGETARIAN FRUIT & NUT-TOPPED CAKE

10 oz/300 g plain wholemeal flour
2 tsp baking powder
I tsp allspice
6 oz/175 g molasses sugar
3 oz/75 g Tomar margarine, softened
4 oz/100 g no-need-to-soak apricots, chopped
6 oz/175 g no-need-to-soak prunes, chopped
2 oz/50 g banana chips, broken
2 oz/50 g sultanas
2 oz/50 g currants
2 oz/50 g ground almonds
2 oz/50 g Brazil nuts, chopped
4 tbsp black treacle
2 tbsp brandy
juice of 3 large oranges
FOR THE TOPPING:
4 tbsp low-sugar apricot jam, sieved
18 Brazil nuts, shelled and skinned
12 no-need-to-soak dried apricots
10 no-need-to-soak dried prunes
12 banana chips

CUTS INTO 24 SLICES
CALORIES PER SLICE: 206

Preheat the oven to Gas 3, 325°F, 160°C. Grease and line a 7 in/18 cm square cake tin with a double layer of lightly greased greaseproof paper. Sieve the wholemeal flour, baking powder and the allspice into a large mixing bowl. Add any bran husks that are left in the sieve. Stir in all remaining cake ingredients and beat thoroughly.

Spoon mixture into the tin and make a small hollow in centre to allow for rising. Bake in the centre of preheated oven for

Enjoy a slice or two of delicious traditional Christmas cake to round off the festive day

2 hrs, or until a skewer inserted in centre of cake comes out clean. Cool in tin for 20 mins, turn on to a rack to cool. Wrap in greaseproof paper and foil, and store in an airtight container for 5-7 days. (Or freeze for up to 2 months until required., allow to thaw thoroughly before decorating.)

To decorate, remove greaseproof paper and foil from the cake and, if necessary, trim the surface of the cake until flat. Place cake on an 8 in/20.5 cm cake board. Heat jam in a bowl over a pan of hot water, stir and brush over top of cake. Arrange the nuts and dried fruit in rows on top of the jam, in a decorative pattern then brush with remaining jam. Cool until thoroughly set.

If liked, attach a ribbon around sides of cake. Eat within 2-3 days of decorating.

TRADITIONAL CHRISTMAS CAKE

12 oz/350 g butter or margarine
12 oz/350 g light soft brown sugar
5 eggs, size 3, beaten
10 oz/300 g plain flour
4 oz/100 g ground almonds
½ tsp ground cinnamon
½ tsp ground ginger
½ tsp ground cloves
½ tsp freshly grated nutmeg
I tbsp black treacle, warmed
grated rind and juice of I lemon
10 oz/300 g sultanas
10 oz/300 g seedless raisins
6 oz/175 g currants
3 oz/75 g chopped mixed nuts
3 oz/75 g glacé cherries, washed, dried and chopped
approx 1½ tbsp brandy or fruit juice
FOR THE ALMOND PASTE:
12 oz/350 g ground almonds
6 oz/175 g caster sugar

remaining flour with the lemon rind and juice, dried fruit, nuts and cherries. Stir thoroughly. Add the remaining flour with the brandy or fruit juice, to give a soft dropping consistency. Turn mixture into prepared cake tin and smooth the top. Make a slight hollow in the centre to ensure a flat cake. Bake towards the bottom of the oven for 2 hrs, then reduce the oven temperature to Gas 1, 275°F, 140°C, and cook the cake for a further 1½-2 hrs or until a skewer inserted into the centre comes out clean. If the top is browning too quickly, cover with greaseproof paper. When cooked remove from the oven and leave in the tin until cold. Remove from tin, store wrapped in greaseproof paper, then foil in a cool, dry place. If liked, prick with a skewer and pour 1-2 tbsp brandy over.

When ready to decorate, discard lining paper. If necessary, trim cake.

Mix the ground almonds and sugars in a bowl, stir in sufficient egg to make a soft but not wet consistency, then add the essences and knead well until smooth.

Wrap in clearwrap.

Heat the jam and lemon juice together, rub through a sieve. Cool, use to glaze surface of cake.

Reserve a third of the almond paste, then divide the remainder into two. On a lightly sugared surface, roll each piece into a strip the depth of the cake and half the circumference. Place around sides of cake, trim and press firmly. Roll out remaining almond paste into a round the same size as the cake. Place on top of the cake. Smooth top and sides using a rolling pin, place on a cake board and leave to dry for three days.

Whisk egg whites until lightly stiff, then whisk in the icing sugar a little at a time. If the texture becomes too stiff add a little of the lemon juice. Whisk in the glycerine. The mixture should be stiff enough for you to form soft peaks with a knife. Cover cake completely. Then make small swirls with a palette knife over the whole cake. Decorate, then leave to set for at least two days.

6 oz/175 g icing sugar, sieved

2 eggs, size 5, beaten

½ tsp vanilla essence

½ tsp almond essence

FOR THE APRICOT GLAZE:

1 tbsp apricot jam

2 tsp lemon juice

FOR THE ROYAL ICING:

3 egg whites, size 3

1½ lb/675 g icing sugar, sifted

1 tbsp lemon juice

1-2 tsp glycerine

MAKES 9 IN/13 CM ROUND CAKE
CALORIES PER PORTION: 586

Preheat the oven to Gas 2, 300°F, 150°C, 10 mins before baking. Grease and line a 9 in/23 cm round cake tin with four layers of greaseproof paper.

Cream the fat and sugar until light and fluffy, then beat in the eggs, adding 1 tbsp of flour after each addition. Add the ground almonds, together with the spices and black treacle. Mix well. Stir in half the

Turn mixture into prepared cake tin, smooth the top

Heat the jam and lemon juice, rub through a sieve. Use to glaze cake

Place the strips of almond paste round the cake, press firmly

Cover cake with royal icing then spread over top and sides

ALTERNATIVE CHRISTMAS PUDDINGS

Christmas would not be Christmas without The Pudding, whether it's the traditional Plum Pudding, rich, dark and full of fruit, a lighter, healthier version or even a frozen Christmas Pudding. All can be served with lashings of cream, brandy butter or rum sauce to make them even more tempting and delicious. Try a new version on your family and enjoy the look of surprise on their faces.

GOLDEN PUDS

Instead of a traditional dark pudding, try these little golden ones – they're lighter in taste and texture and have a wonderful aroma of cinnamon.

3 oz/75 g fresh brown breadcrumbs
2 oz/50 g shredded vegetable suet
pinch of salt
1 tsp ground cinnamon
½ tsp ground ginger
2 oz/50 g light soft brown sugar
3 oz/75 g chopped mixed peel
3 oz/75 g no-need-to-soak apricots, chopped
3 oz/75 g sultanas
2 eggs, size 4, beaten
1½ tbsp golden syrup, warmed
1 tbsp brandy
approx 1 tbsp milk

MAKES FOUR ¼ PINT/150 ML INDIVIDUAL PUDDINGS • CALORIES PER PORTION: 435

Grease and line four ¼ pint/150 ml individual pudding basins. Mix all the dry ingredients together in a large bowl. In another bowl, beat together all remaining ingredients, except milk. Stir into dry mixture, adding enough milk to give a soft but not runny consistency.

Pack mixture into basins leaving a gap at the top to allow for expansion. Cover each pudding tightly with foil, then steam steadily for 3 hrs. Remove from steamer and allow to cool. Recover and store. Steam for a further 1 hr before serving.

CANDIED PUD

This is a variation on the traditional Christmas pud – packed with delicious candied fruits.

4 oz/100 g fresh brown breadcrumbs
8 oz/225 g plain flour
1 oz/25 g natural wheat bran
½ tsp salt
8 oz/225 g shredded vegetable suet
1 tsp ground mace
½ tsp ground ginger
½ tsp ground cinnamon
½ tsp ground nutmeg
8 oz/225 g light soft brown sugar
6 oz/175 g chopped mixed peel
6 oz/175 g sultanas
4 oz/100 g glacé cherries, washed, dried and chopped
2 oz/50 g stem ginger, washed dried and chopped
8 oz/225 g apple, peeled, cored and grated
grated rind and juice of 1 orange
3-4 tbsp brandy or fruit juice
3 eggs, size 3, beaten
approx 6 tbsp milk

MAKES TWO 1½ PINT/900 ML PUDDINGS CALORIES PER PORTION: 475

Grease and line base of two 1½ pint/900 ml pudding basins. Proceed as for Golden Pud, and pack down mixture firmly in basins. Cover each pudding with a pudding cloth or a double sheet of foil with a pleat in centre. Secure firmly. Steam steadily for 7 hrs.

Cool completely, then re-cover and store. Steam the pudding for a further 3 hrs before serving.

FROZEN PUD

Try this frozen pud as a change from the traditional steamed one. You can vary the fruits and liquor according to your taste.

1 pint/600 ml milk
6 egg yolks, size 3
4 oz/100 g caster sugar
3 tbsp medium-sweet sherry
1 pint/600 ml whipping cream, lightly whipped
3 oz/75 g dark chocolate, melted
1 oz/25 g chocolate chips
2 oz/50 g raisins
2 oz/50 g sultanas
1 oz/25 g chopped mixed peel
1 oz/25 g glacé cherries, washed, dried and chopped
1 oz/25 g angelica, washed, dried and chopped

MAKES 2½ PINT/1.5 LITRE PUDDING; SERVES 12 • CALORIES PER PORTION: 357

Set freezer to rapid-freeze 2 hrs before making ice-cream. Warm the milk to blood heat in a pan, remove from heat. Beat the egg yolks with the sugar until pale and creamy, then beat in the milk. Strain into a clean pan, then cook over a gentle heat until mixture thickens and coats the back of a wooden spoon. Pour into a container and freeze for 1½ hrs, stirring occasionally.

Place mixture in a bowl and fold in the sherry and whipped cream. Spoon a quarter of the mixture into a small bowl, then add melted chocolate and stir thoroughly. Fold in chocolate chips, then pour into a small container and freeze. Add

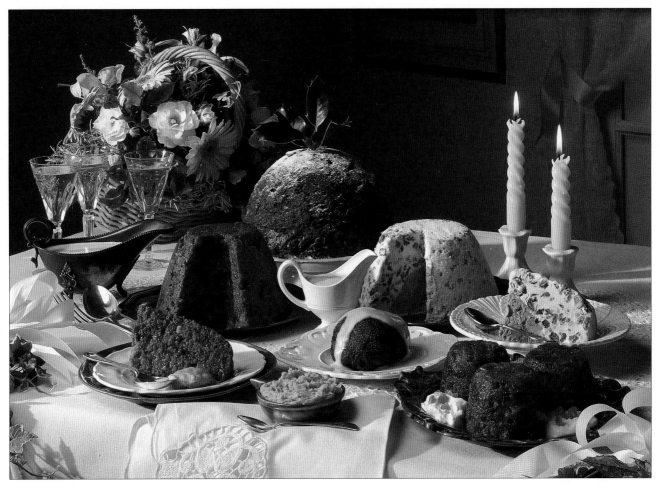

Clockwise from left: Candied Pud with Brandy Butter; Traditional Pud, served with cream; Frozen Pud; Golden Puds with Candied Cheese; Baby Pud with Rum Sauce

dried fruit, peel, cherries and angelica to the remaining mixture, then freeze for a further 40 mins.

Remove both mixtures from freezer, beat well, then freeze the chocolate ice-cream again.

Place the white ice-cream into a 2½ pint/1.5 litre pudding basin, moulding the mixture around the sides and bottom of the bowl and hollowing out the centre. Return to the freezer for a further 1 hr. Remove chocolate ice-cream from freezer and allow to soften slightly, then use to fill the hollow in the centre of the white ice-cream. Smooth the top, cover, then freeze until required. (Don't forget to turn freezer setting back to its normal temperature.) Before serving, allow to soften for about 30 mins in the fridge.

TRADITIONAL PUD

This rich fruity pud is the nearest thing to the traditional Plum Pudding of years ago.

4 oz/100 g fresh brown breadcrumbs
4 oz/100 g fine oatmeal
12 oz/350 g plain white flour
1 level tsp salt
8 oz/225 g shredded vegetable suet
12 oz/350 g muscovado sugar
3 tsp mixed spice
8 oz/225 g currants
8 oz/225 g chopped dates
1 lb /450 g seedless raisins
4 oz/100 g no-need-to-soak prunes, chopped
3 tbsp black treacle
grated rind and juice of 2 lemons
5 eggs, size 3, beaten
2 tbsp brandy or rum
approx 4-6 tbsp fruit juice or milk
icing sugar and holly to decorate

MAKES 4 PINT/2.25 LITRE PUDDING; SERVES 24 • CALORIES PER PORTION: 341

Grease a 4 pint/2.25 litre round Christmas pudding mould. Alternatively, use a pudding cloth.

In a large basin, mix together the breadcrumbs, oatmeal, flour, salt, suet and sugar. Add spice then the dried fruit and mix lightly. Stir in the treacle, lemon rind and juice and eggs. Beat to a soft dropping consistency with brandy or rum and fruit juice or milk.

Pack into the 2 halves of the mould, fix mould together and place on stand. If using pudding cloth, lightly dust with flour, place mixture in centre, shape into a round and tie firmly. Place mould in a large pan with enough water to come halfway up sides. Cook steadily for 9 hrs, topping up with boiling water as necessary.

If using a pudding cloth, you can steam the pudding in a steamer for 9 hrs. Alternatively, cook as for mould. Cool, then re-cover and store.

Steam for a further 4 hrs before serving, sprinkled with icing sugar and decorated with holly.

Serve this delicious round Christmas Pudding with cream, serve fresh fruit to follow

BABY PUDS

By using breadcrumbs alone with no suet, a much lighter-textured pudding is achieved. It won't keep quite as long as a suet pud but will keep in a dark, airy place or in the fridge for up to 3 weeks.

8 oz/225 g butter or margarine
4 oz/100 g light soft brown sugar
4 oz/100 g muscovado sugar
3 eggs, size 5
3 oz/75 g self-raising flour
8 oz/225 g currants
8 oz/225 g sultanas
8 oz/225 g raisins
8 oz/225 g chopped dates
1 lb/450 g seedless raisins
4 oz/100 g no-need-to-soak apricots, chopped
1 tsp ground cinnamon
1 tsp mixed spice
grated rind and juice of 1 orange
2 tbsp golden syrup, warmed
9 oz/250 g fresh brown breadcrumbs

MAKES 8 • CALORIES PER PUDDING: 799

Cream fat with the sugars until light and fluffy, then beat in eggs alternately with the flour. Add the dried fruit and mix thoroughly. Sprinkle in the spices and orange rind, mix well, then add the orange juice and syrup.

Fold in the breadcrumbs to give a fairly stiff consistency. Have ready eight small squares of muslin or clean cloth. Divide mixture between them, placing it in the centre of each. Twist each cloth to encase the mixture completely, forming small round puddings.

Enclose each pudding in a square of foil and twist to seal. Place in the top of a steamer, steam steadily for 3 hrs. Cool, re-cover and store. Steam for a further 1 hr before serving.

Alternatively use small dariole moulds. Lightly grease moulds and line bases with greaseproof paper.

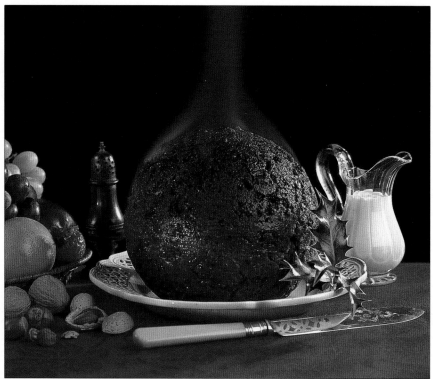

ROUND CHRISTMAS PUDDING

6 oz/175 g carrots
6 oz/175 g no-need-to-soak pitted prunes
2 lemons, preferably unwaxed
8 oz/225 g unsalted butter
8 oz/225 g dark muscovado sugar
6 eggs, size 3, beaten
6 oz/175 g self-raising flour, sieved
3 tbsp cane molasses or black treacle
1 tsp freshly grated nutmeg
1 tsp ground cinnamon
½ tsp ground cloves
8 oz/225 g raisins
8 oz/225 g currants
8 oz/225 g sultanas
4 oz/100 g chopped mixed peel
8 oz/225 g fresh brown breadcrumbs
2-3 tbsp brandy, sherry or orange juice
2-3 tbsp brandy (optional) to serve
holly sprig to decorate

SERVES 16 • CALORIES PER PORTION: 425

Peel and coarsely grate the carrots, then reserve. Using scissors or a sharp knife, cut the prunes into small pieces. Finely grate the rind from the lemons. Cream the butter and sugar until pale and creamy, then beat in lemon rind.

Add the eggs, a little at a time, with 1 tbsp flour, beating well after each addition. Stir in cane molasses or black treacle. Fold in the remaining flour and spices, then add grated carrots and dried fruit, including peel and prunes. Mix well. Stir in breadcrumbs, juice from lemons, and enough brandy, sherry or orange juice to give a soft dropping consistency. Cover loosely and leave in a cool place overnight.

Cut out two circles of greaseproof paper, approx 4 in/10 cm in diameter, then make four to five 1½ in/4 cm slits towards centre of each circle (this helps it to curve into mould). Lightly grease a round Christmas pudding mould, place a paper circle in each half, then brush with oil. Divide the pudding mixture between halves, then fit them together. Put mould in its stand, then place in a large saucepan half-filled with boiling water. Steam for 8 hrs, replenishing water as needed. Remove from pan and leave to cool.

Store in a cool, dry place. When ready to use, re-steam for 4 hrs. Heat brandy if using, then pour over pudding and ignite immediately. Decorate and serve.

Peel and grate the carrots. Snip the prunes into very small pieces and reserve

Cream the butter and sugar until pale and creamy, then beat in the grated lemon rind

Stir in the cane molasses or black treacle and beat well until thoroughly mixed

Fold in flour, spices and carrots, dried fruit and prunes. Stir in the bread-crumbs

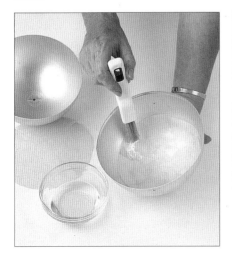

Lightly grease a round Christmas pudding mould and place a circle of paper in each

Divide the pudding mixture between each half of the mould then fit them together

CANDIED CHEESE

8oz/250 ml fromage frais
sugar to taste
1-2 tbsp sweet sherry (optional)
1 oz/25 g chopped mixed peel

MAKES ½ PINT/300 ML
CALORIES PER 1 FL OZ/25 ML: 25

Combine all the ingredients and place in a serving dish. Cover, then chill until required. Serve with Golden Puds.

RUM SAUCE

½ pint/300 ml milk
1 egg, size 3
1 egg yolk, size 3
2 tbsp caster sugar
2 tbsp rum
½ oz/15 g butter

MAKES ¾ PINT/450 ML • SERVES 0
CALORIES PER 1 FL OZ/25 ML: 40

Warm the milk to blood heat in a pan. Beat together the egg, egg yolk and sugar in a bowl until pale and creamy, then gradually beat in the warmed milk. Strain into a clean pan, then cook over a very gentle heat, stirring throughout until the mixture thickens to the point where it coats the back of a wooden spoon. Remove from heat, then add rum and butter. Stir until butter has melted. Cover with dampened greaseproof paper to prevent a skin forming. Serve hot or cold.

BRANDY BUTTER

6 oz/175 g unsalted butter, softened
3 oz/75 g caster sugar
3 oz/75 g light soft brown sugar
4-5 tbsp brandy

MAKES ½ LB/225 G
CALORIES PER 1 OZ/25 G: 254

Cream the butter until pale and creamy. Gradually add the sugars, beating between each addition, then add the brandy, a little at a time, to ensure the mixture doesn't curdle. Pile into a dish and chill. Keep, covered, in a fridge for up to 1 week. To keep longer, freeze until needed.

FESTIVE PASTRIES

Following a few simple steps, you can bake the best pastries ever! Puff pastries that are mouthwateringly good, crisp light shortcrust, tempting choux buns filled with choc'n'orange cream...these and many more delights are in store for you when you cook these delicious recipes!

SHORTCRUST PASTRY

8 oz/225 g plain white flour
pinch of salt
2 oz/50 g butter or margarine
2 oz/50 g white vegetable fat

MAKES 8 OZ/225 G
CALORIES PER 1 OZ/25 G: 129

Sieve flour and salt into a mixing bowl. Cut the fats into small cubes, add to flour, then rub in until mixture resembles fine bread-crumbs. Mix with 3-4 tbsp cold water to form a firm but pliable dough.

Turn out on to a lightly floured surface and knead until smooth and free from cracks. Wrap in greaseproof paper and allow the pastry to relax for 30 mins. **Note:** If the pastry is not allowed to relax, it will shrink on cooking.

PUFF PASTRY

8 oz/225 g plain white flour
pinch of salt
8 oz/225 g unsalted butter
squeeze of lemon juice

MAKES 8 OZ/225 G
CALORIES PER 1 OZ/25 G: 115

Preheat the oven to Gas 7, 425°F, 220°C, 15 mins before baking.

Sieve flour and salt into a bowl. Rub 1 oz/25 g butter into flour, then mix to a soft dough with lemon juice and about 3-4 tbsp chilled water. Shape remaining butter into an oblong. Roll dough out to an oblong, three times as long as butter. Place butter in centre of dough. Bring top third down over butter and bottom third up. Seal edges lightly with a rolling pin. Wrap and leave to rest in fridge for 30 mins.

Place the dough with sealed edges at top and bottom, then roll, fold and relax the pastry. Repeat process once more, then leave to relax in the fridge for at least 3 hrs before using.

CHOUX PASTRY

2 oz/50 g unsalted butter
3 oz/75 g plain white flour, sieved
2 eggs, size 2, beaten

MAKES 6 OZ/175 G
CALORIES PER 1 OZ/25 G: 61

Preheat the oven to Gas 6, 400°F, 200°C, 15 mins before baking. Melt the butter in a pan with ¼ pint/150 ml water over a gentle heat. Remove from heat, tip in all the flour, then beat with a wooden spoon until mixture forms a ball in the centre of the pan.

Gradually add the eggs, beating vigorously after each addition. (It is important to beat vigorously to trap in as much air as possible.) Continue beating until the mixture is smooth and glossy. Place in a piping bag and pipe small rounds on to a dampened baking sheet. Bake for 15-20 mins, or until well risen. Make a small slit in the sides or base of each bun so that steam can escape, then return to the oven for 5 mins to dry out the buns. Remove and cool on a wire rack.

HOT WATER CRUST PASTRY

1 lb/450 g plain white flour
1 tsp salt
4 oz/100 g white vegetable fat

MAKES 1 LB/450 G
CALORIES PER 1 OZ/25 G: 129

Sieve flour and salt into a bowl. Melt fat with 9 fl oz/275 ml water, bring to the boil. Pour on to flour. Beat until mixture forms a ball in the centre of the bowl. When the mixture is cool enough to handle, knead dough lightly until smooth. Place in a clean bowl, cover and leave for 10 mins. Use as required but do not allow to become cold before shaping.

EMPANADAS WITH SPICY TOMATO SAUCE

FOR THE TOMATO SAUCE:
1 tbsp olive oil
1 small onion, chopped
1 garlic clove, peeled and crushed
1 small red chilli, deseeded and chopped
8 oz/225 g ripe tomatoes, peeled
1-2 tbsp tomato purée
1 tsp sugar
few dashes Tabasco sauce
1 small green chilli, deseeded
FOR THE EMPANADAS:
4 oz/100 g ground beef
1 tbsp chopped onion
1 garlic clove, peeled and crushed
1 tbsp red pepper, chopped
1 tbsp freshly chopped coriander
salt and freshly ground black pepper
2 tbsp beef or vegetable stock
4 oz/100 g prepared Shortcrust Pastry
oil for deep-frying
fresh coriander sprigs to garnish

SERVES 4 • CALORIES PER PORTION: 368

For the sauce, heat olive oil, then gently fry the onion, garlic and red chilli for 3 mins. Deseed tomatoes, chop, add to the pan and simmer gently for 5 mins, stirring

Bottom: Fruity Twists (made with Puff Pastry); Middle: Greek Yogurt Flan (Shortcrust Pastry); Top: Empanadas (Shortcrust Pastry), served with Spicy Tomato Sauce

occasionally. Add tomato purée to taste, stir in the sugar and Tabasco. Slice green chilli, reserving a few rings for garnish, then chop remainder and stir into sauce. Cook for a further 5 mins, or until sauce reaches a thick consistency. Transfer to a jug, garnish with reserved chilli rings and serve hot or cold.

For the empanadas, place beef, onion, garlic and red pepper in a non-stick frying pan, dry-fry gently for 5-7 mins, stirring occasionally until beef is browned. Add the chopped coriander, seasoning and stock. Continue to cook gently for a further 5-7 mins, then cool.

Roll out pastry, cut into eight 3 in/7.5 cm rounds. Place a spoonful of filling on each, dampen edges then fold over and pinch together. Heat oil to 350°F, 180°C. Fry empanadas a few at a time for 4-5 mins, or until golden. Drain well, garnish and serve with the tomato sauce.

GREEK YOGURT FLAN

4 oz/100 g prepared Shortcrust pastry
3 tbsp clear honey
1 tsp ground ginger
1 lb/450 g Greek set yogurt
4 tbsp icing sugar, sieved
3 oz/75 g stem ginger
2-3 fresh figs

SERVES 4 • CALORIES PER PORTION: 316

Preheat the oven to Gas 6, 400°F, 200°C, 15 mins before baking the flan case. Line an 8 in/20.5 cm fluted flan ring with the prepared pastry, allow it to relax for 30 mins, then bake blind for 15 mins, or until the pastry is cooked. Remove from the oven and leave until cold.

Remove flan ring, place pastry case on to a serving plate. Mix together the honey and ginger and use to cover base of flan.

Mix together the Greek yogurt and icing sugar, then spoon over honey and ginger mixture. Decorate flan with ginger and figs.

FRUITY TWISTS

2 oz/50 g butter or margarine
2 oz/50 g light soft brown sugar
1 tsp ground cinnamon
3 oz/75 g mixed dried fruit
1 lb/450 g prepared Puff Pastry
1 oz/25 g caster sugar

MAKES 16 • CALORIES PER PORTION: 95

Preheat the oven to Gas 7, 425°F, 220°C, 15 mins before baking. Cream together the fat, sugar and cinnamon, then mix in dried fruit.

Cut the prepared pastry in half. Roll out one half and cut out eight 3 in/7.5 cm squares. Halve the filling and divide it equally between the squares, placing a small spoonful of filling just off centre.

Dampen the edges with a little water. Then, starting from the bottom right-hand corner, roll up the pastry, making sure you encase the filling. Bring the ends round to form a crescent and pinch the edges together firmly.

Roll out the remaining pastry, then cut out eight 3 in/7.5 cm squares. Divide remaining filling between squares, placing a small spoonful in the centre of each. Dampen the edges, then fold from corner to corner to form triangles. Flute the edges firmly together.

Brush the crescents and triangles with a little water and sprinkle evenly with the caster sugar. Place on dampened baking sheets and bake in the preheated oven for 10-15 mins, or until well risen and golden brown. They are best eaten while still warm.

CHICKEN PIES

1 lb/450 g prepared Hot Water
    Crust Pastry
FOR THE FILLING:
3 oz/75 g cooked chicken or turkey
    meat, without the bones or skin
½ small red pepper
2 oz/50 g sweetcorn, thawed if
    frozen, drained if canned
3 oz/75 g broccoli florets
8 fl oz/250 ml prepared thick
    white sauce
1 scant tsp ground mace
salt and freshly ground black
    pepper
1 egg, size 5, beaten

SERVES 4 • CALORIES PER PORTION: 536

Preheat the oven to Gas 7, 425°F, 220°C, 15 mins before baking the pies. Divide pastry into four, then mould over the bases of four greased jam jars, reserving sufficient pastry for lids. While pastry cases are setting, make the filling.

For the filling, chop meat into small chunks, then place in a bowl. Deseed pepper and chop finely, add to bowl with sweetcorn. Wash and blanch broccoli, chop, add to bowl. Mix in the white sauce with the mace and seasoning.

Carefully remove pastry cases from the

HANDY TIPS

If preferred you can make one large chicken pie instead of individual ones.
Roll out two-thirds of the Hot Water Crust Pastry on a lightly floured surface and use to line an 8 in/20.5 cm spring form release tin. Carefully mould the pastry into the sides and base of the tin so that there are no gaps. Cover pastry while preparing the filling.
Pack the filling into the tin then roll out the remaining pastry to form the lid. Brush the edges of the pastry with a little beaten egg and press together firmly.
Bake at Gas 7, 425°F, 220°C for 30 mins. Reduce the temperature to Gas 4, 350°F, 180°C and cook for a further 1-1¼ hrs.

jam jars, then fill cases with prepared mixture. Roll out four lids from reserved pastry and place in position. Pinch the edges firmly together. Roll out trimmings and use to decorate pie lids. Place on a lightly greased baking sheet and brush pastry with some of the egg. Make a small hole in the centre of pies to allow steam to escape.

Bake in oven for 15 mins, then brush pies again with more egg. Reduce the oven temperature to Gas 4, 350°F, 180°C, and continue to bake for 20 mins, or until the pies are golden brown.

Serve hot with fresh vegetables or cold with a crisp salad.

FISH PIE

1 lb/450 g white fish fillets, such as
    whiting, pollock or cod, skinned
½ pint/300 ml fish stock
4 fl oz/120 ml medium-dry white
    wine or extra stock
a few saffron strands
1½ oz/40 g butter or margarine
1½ oz/40 g plain white flour
salt and freshly ground black pepper
3 tbsp single cream
3 tbsp milk
4 oz/100 g peeled prawns, thawed
    if frozen
8 oz/225 g tomatoes, peeled and
    chopped
8 oz/225 g prepared Shortcrust Pastry
1 egg, size 5, beaten

SERVES 4 • CALORIES PER PORTION: 742

Preheat the oven to Gas 6, 400°F, 200°C, 15 mins before baking pie.

Wash fish, place in a frying pan, cover with stock and poach gently for 12 mins, or until cooked. Drain, reserving ¼ pint/150 ml stock. Flake fish and reserve.

Pour reserved stock into a small pan. Add wine or extra stock and saffron, bring to boil, then simmer for 1 min. Strain liquid, return to pan and bring to boil. Beat together fat and flour to make a beurre manié, then whisk small spoonfuls into the boiling liquid. Continue whisking and adding beurre manié until sauce is smooth and glossy.

Remove from heat, season then add cream and milk. Stir in reserved fish, prawns and tomatoes, then turn mixture into a 2 pint/1.2 litre oval pie dish.

On a lightly floured surface, roll out prepared pastry to an oval 1 in/2.5 cm larger than pie dish. Cut out a 1 in/2.5 cm strip, dampen pie dish lip and place pastry strip on top. Dampen strip, cover pie with pastry to form a lid. Pinch edges firmly together. Roll out trimmings and use to decorate pie. Brush with some of the beaten egg, then bake for 15 mins. Brush again with egg and cook for a further 15 mins, or until pastry is golden brown.

VEGETABLE TRANCHE

8 oz/225 g prepared Puff Pastry
1 egg, size 5, beaten
FOR THE FILLING:
6 oz/175 g potatoes
4 oz/100 g carrots
2-3 tbsp semi-skimmed milk
salt and freshly ground black
    pepper
1 onion
1 tbsp oil
3 oz/75 g broccoli florets
3 oz/75 g cauliflower florets
FOR THE SAUCE:
8 oz/225 g fromage frais
1-2 garlic cloves, peeled and crushed
2 tbsp freshly snipped chives
fresh sage sprigs to garnish

SERVES 4 • CALORIES PER PORTION: 749

Preheat the oven to Gas 7, 425°F, 220°C, 15 mins before baking the tranche. Roll out the prepared puff pastry to ½ in/1.25 cm thick. Cut out a 10 in x 6 in/25.5 cm x 15 cm oblong. Cut off a ½ in/1.25 cm strip from the oblong, brush a little of the beaten egg on the underside of the strip, then place on the edge of the oblong to form a border.

Place the oblong on a baking sheet and flute the edges together. Prick inside of tranche and brush edge with more beaten egg. Bake for 20 mins, or until the pastry is well risen and golden brown.

Meanwhile prepare the filling. Peel

potatoes and carrots, cut into chunks, then cook in boiling salted water for 15 mins, or until soft. Drain vegetables, then mash with milk and seasoning. Keep warm.

Peel the onion and chop finely. Heat oil, cook onion for 5 mins, then mix into mash. Wash broccoli and cauliflower, divide into tiny florets, blanch in boiling salted water for 4 mins, then drain.

To prepare sauce, mix together the fromage frais, garlic and chives and place in a serving jug.

Fill cooked pastry case with the prepared mash, then top the broccoli and cauliflower florets. Garnish and serve with the prepared sauce.

CHOC'N'ORANGE PUFFS

6 oz/175 g prepared Choux Pastry buns
FOR THE FILLING:
1 large or 2 medium oranges
½ pint/300 ml whipping cream
2 oz/50 g plain chocolate, grated
1 tsp icing sugar

MAKES 16 • CALORIES PER PORTION: 77

Halve the prepared buns and set aside. Finely grate rind from half the large orange or from 1 medium orange. Peel the orange (or both if using 2). Remove as much bitter white pith as possible, then divide the fruit into segments. Whip the cream until thick, fold in the orange rind and chocolate, then place in a piping bag.

Divide orange segments between choux bun bases, top with cream. Place lids of buns in position, sieve a little icing sugar over and serve immediately.

Clockwise from bottom: Chicken Pie (Hot Water Crust Pastry); Vegetable Tranche (Puff Pastry), served with a sauce of fromage frais, garlic and chives; Fish Pie (Shortcrust Pastry); and Choc'n'Orange Puffs (Choux Pastry)

TIPSY RECIPES

Carry on the season of goodwill by adding a drop of Christmas cheer to your cooking. Serve your family and friends these deliciously tipsy recipes throughout the festive season.

BEETROOT SOUP

2 lb/900 g raw beetroot, trimmed of
   leaves, washed and peeled
2 onions, peeled and chopped
2 pint/1.2 litres vegetable or chicken
   stock
juice of 1 lemon
½ pint/300 ml red wine
salt and freshly ground black pepper
2 tbsp arrowroot
4 tsp soured cream
fresh chives to garnish

SERVES 4 • CALORIES PER PORTION: 104

Grate the beetroot, then place in a large saucepan with the onions, vegetable or chicken stock, lemon juice and red wine. Add seasoning, bring to the boil, then simmer gently for 15 mins. Cool slightly, blend in a processor for a few seconds, then pass through a fine sieve to form a smooth purée. Return to rinsed pan and reheat.

Blend the arrowroot and 2 tbsp cold water to form a smooth paste. Stir paste into the beetroot soup and cook, stirring throughout, until slightly thickened.

To serve, divide the soup between bowls, swirl a little soured cream into each garnish with chives. Serve hot or chilled.

PLAICE WITH VERMOUTH

4 large plaice fillets, each weighing
about 6 oz/175 g, skinned
salt and freshly ground black pepper
1 courgette
½ pint/300 ml fish or vegetable stock
3-4 tbsp dry vermouth
1 oz/25 g butter or margarine
1 oz/25 g plain white flour
2 tbsp fromage frais
freshly cooked spinach, chopped
seedless green grapes, halved and
   quartered lemon slices to garnish

SERVES 4 • CALORIES PER PORTION: 242

Preheat the oven to Gas 4, 350°F, 180°C, 10 mins before cooking the plaice. Cut the plaice fillets in half lengthways, then wash lightly and dry on kitchen paper. Place the fillets skinned side down on a chopping board and season to taste.

Wash and dry courgette, then, using a vegetable peeler, shave very thin slices lengthways. Place two slices of courgette lengthways on each fillet and, starting from the widest end, carefully roll up.

Place the rolled-up fillets in a shallow ovenproof dish, then pour the stock and vermouth over the top. Cover and cook in the oven for 15-20 mins, or until fish is cooked. Drain the cooking liquid from the fish into a small pan, then cover the fish and keep warm.

Make a beurre manié by beating together the fat and flour. Bring the cook-

Clockwise from bottom left: tasty Plaice with Vermouth, garnished with grapes and lemon; Beetroot Soup, served with a swirl of soured cream; mouthwatering Pavlova; Pork Chops with Madeira Sauce, served with vegetables; and centre, tempting Tipsy Parson

ing liquid to the boil, then drop small spoonfuls of the beurre manié into the liquid, whisking well after each addition. When sauce is thick, smooth and glossy, add the fromage frais and adjust the seasoning, if necessary.

Place the freshly cooked spinach over the base of a serving dish, then arrange the rolled fillets on top. Spoon a little of the prepared sauce over the fish, then garnish with the halved grapes and quartered lemon slices. Serve the remaining sauce separately.

PORK CHOPS WITH MADEIRA SAUCE

4 boneless pork chops, each weighing about 6 oz/175 g
freshly ground white pepper
1 tsp oil
FOR THE MADEIRA SAUCE:
¼ pint/150 ml unsweetened orange juice
1 oz/25 g soft brown sugar
3 oz/75 g cranberries, thawed if frozen
3 fl oz/85 ml Madeira
3 tsp cornflour
fresh chervil sprigs to garnish

SERVES 4 • CALORIES PER PORTION: 454

Preheat the grill to high. Season each chop with the freshly ground white pepper, then brush both sides with a little oil. Place the chops under the grill and cook for 2 mins on both sides. Reduce the heat to moderate and continue to grill the chops, turning them halfway through cooking, for 15-20 mins, or until cooked.

Meanwhile, make the Madeira sauce. Pour the unsweetened orange juice into a small saucepan, then add the soft brown sugar, cranberries and Madeira. Bring to the boil, then reduce the heat and simmer for 8 mins, or until the cranberries have softened.

Blend the cornflour with 1 tbsp cold water to form a smooth paste, then add to the cranberries in the pan and cook, stirring throughout, until the sauce has thickened.

Garnish chops with fresh chervil sprigs

and serve with a selection of freshly cooked seasonal vegetables and the Madeira sauce.

PAVLOVA

4 egg whites, size 3
8 oz/225 g caster sugar
1 tsp vanilla essence
1 tsp vinegar
FOR THE FILLING:
8 oz/225 g chestnut purée
4 oz/100 g plain dark chocolate
4 tbsp medium-sweet sherry
6 tbsp extra-thick double cream
1 oz/25 g chopped skinned hazelnuts
½ oz/15 g flaked almonds

SERVES 8 • CALORIES PER PORTION: 367

Preheat the oven to Gas 6, 400°F, 200°C, 15 mins before cooking the pavlova. Whisk the egg whites until stiff and peaking, then gradually whisk in the caster sugar, 1 tbsp at a time, whisking well after each addition. When all the sugar has been added, fold in the vanilla essence and vinegar.

Line a baking sheet with vegetable parchment paper. Place the meringue mixture in a large piping bag fitted with a large star nozzle and pipe a 5 in/12.5 cm circle on to the lined baking sheet. Pipe round the circle to form a 2 in/5 cm high edge. Reduce the oven temperature to Gas 1, 275°F, 140°C, and cook the meringue for 2 hrs, or until set. Remove from the oven and leave to cool.

Meanwhile, make the filling. Beat the chestnut purée until softened. Break the plain dark chocolate into small pieces and place in a small heatproof bowl with the sherry. Place the bowl over a pan of gently simmering water, and stir occasionally until chocolate is smooth and completely melted.

Remove from the heat, then beat chocolate mixture into the chestnut purée. Beat mixture until smooth and cold. Add the double cream and fold in until thoroughly mixed. Stir in the chopped hazelnuts, then leave in the fridge to thicken.

When ready to serve the pavlova, care-

fully spoon the prepared chilled filling into the cold meringue case, then decorate the filling with flaked almonds.

TIPSY PARSON

4 oz/100 g unsalted butter, softened
4 oz/100 g caster sugar
2 tbsp strong black coffee
5 tbsp Grand Marnier
8 trifle sponge cakes
15 oz/425 g can mango slices, drained
½ pint/300 ml whipping cream
orange zest to decorate

SERVES 8 • CALORIES PER PORTION: 420

Line the base and both ends of a 2 pint/1.2 litre loaf tin with lightly oiled vegetable parchment paper.

Cream together the softened butter and the caster sugar until light and fluffy, then gradually beat in the strong black coffee and 3 tbsp Grand Marnier.

Arrange 4 trifle sponge cakes in the base of the lined loaf tin, drizzle 1 tbsp remaining Grand Marnier over the sponge, then spread half the butter mixture on the top. Arrange the drained mango slices over the butter mixture, then top with the remaining sponge cakes. Drizzle remaining Grand Marnier over, and spread with the remaining butter mixture. Cover with a sheet of greaseproof paper, then weigh down with weights or wiped cans. Chill overnight.

Remove the weights and paper, then turn cake out on to a serving dish. Whip the cream until thick, then spoon two-thirds on to the cake. Using a palette knife, smooth the cream over the top and sides of the cake. Place the remaining cream in a piping bag and use to decorate top and sides. Decorate top with the orange zest.

HANDY TIPS

After enjoying a glass of wine with your family and friends, save any leftover wine to flavour casseroles, stews and gravies. Don't forget to cork the wine as soon as possible and store in a cool place in your kitchen.

PRESENTS TO MAKE

Here is a collection of easy gifts to make at home. Daintily decorated and prettily packaged, they make very special presents for you to give with love.

CHRISTMAS LANTERNS

Brighten up your Christmas tree by making these fun Christmas Lanterns. Make them 1-2 weeks before Christmas then attach them to the tree with brightly coloured ribbons

2 oz/50 g soft dark brown sugar
2 oz/50 g black treacle
pinch of ground cinnamon
pinch of ground cloves
pinch of ground ginger
1½ oz/40 g butter
¾ tsp bicarbonate of soda
8 oz/225 g plain flour
1 egg, size 5, separated
6 red clear boiled sweets
4 each of red, yellow, mauve and green clear boiled fruit sweets
pink ribbon for finishing

MAKES 8 • CALORIES PER LANTERN 199

Preheat the oven to Gas 4, 350°F, 180°C, 10 mins before baking. Place the sugar, treacle, spices and fat in a saucepan and heat gently until melted. Remove from the heat. Blend the bicarbonate of soda with 1 tsp cold water and add to the pan with the flour, and egg yolk.

Mix to a soft dough, knead on a lightly floured surface until smooth.

Roll the dough out onto a lightly floured surface and cut out thirty-two 2 in/5 cm squares.

Carefully cut the centre from each square, leaving a ½ in/1.25 cm frame. Place on two baking sheets, lined with baking parchment paper. Knead all the trimmings together, reserve.

Cut the sweets in half and place a piece of each colour inside each frame. Bake in the oven for 15-20 mins or until the sweets have melted and filled the

Above: pretty Christmas Lanterns; ideal Christmas tree decorations that are fun and easy to make

frames. Leave to cool completely and then carefully remove from the paper.

Roll out the trimmings to a 10 in/25 cm square, and cut out sixteen 2½ in/6.5 cm squares. Using the widest end of a ½ in/1.25 cm piping nozzle, cut out eight circles from the remaining trimmings. Cut out the centres of the circles with the narrow end of the nozzle. Place the squares and rings on a lightly floured baking sheet and cook as before.

Place the remaining red sweets and 1 tsp of water in a bowl over a pan of boiling water until melted.

Using a cocktail stick, spread the edges of four biscuits with different coloured centres with melted sweets and press together to make a square. If preferred, stick lanterns together with royal icing. Attach a solid square biscuit to the top and bottom. Attach a ring to the top of the lantern. Repeat to form eight lanterns. Tie the ribbon through the rings on top of the lanterns and wrap in clearwrap to store if required.

NUT CLUSTERS

8 oz/225 g plain or milk chocolate
1 oz/25 g butter
4 oz/100 g ground almonds
4 oz/100 g lightly crushed flaked almonds

MAKES 20 • CALORIES PER CLUSTER: 134

Break up the chocolate and place in a heatproof bowl over a pan of hot water, heat until melted. Remove from heat and beat in the butter and ground and crushed flaked almonds. Place the mixture in the fridge for about 30 mins. Form into twenty clusters, place in petit four cases.

CHOCOLATE TRUFFLES

8 oz/225 g cake crumbs
1 oz/25 g ground almonds
1 oz/25 g melted plain chocolate
finely grated rind of 1 orange
3-4 tbsp dark rum or milk chocolate vermicelli
2 oz/50 g sieved icing sugar

MAKES 20 • CALORIES PER TRUFFLE: 65

Place cake crumbs, ground almonds, melted chocolate and orange rind in a bowl. Bind together with the rum or milk. Divide mixture into 20 portions, roll into balls. Toss 10 truffles in chocolate vermicelli and the other 10 in sieved icing sugar. Place truffles in petit four cases and pack in boxes.

CHRISTMAS TREE DECORATIONS

5 oz/150 g plain flour
1 oz/25 g cornflour
3 oz/75 g butter
1 oz/25 g vanilla sugar
3-4 tbsp milk
FOR THE DECORATION:
8 oz/225 g fondant icing
honey for brushing
assorted food colourings

MAKES 16 • CALORIES PER BISCUIT: 138

Preheat the oven to Gas 5, 375°F, 190°C. Sieve the flour and cornflour into a bowl. Rub in the butter until it resembles bread-crumbs. Stir in the vanilla sugar and bind with the milk to form a firm dough. Roll out on a lightly floured surface. Using a 2½ in/6.5 cm fluted cutter, stamp out sixteen shapes. Place on a greased baking sheet, cook in the oven for 15-20 mins. Cool on a wire rack. Roll out the fondant icing and, using a 2 in/5 cm flower-shaped cutter, stamp out sixteen shapes. Brush the biscuits with honey and secure a flower on each. Using a skewer, make a small hole to thread ribbon through.

Colour the remaining fondant with food colouring and make holly, Christmas trees, and parcels. Secure these on top of fondant covered biscuits with water. Allow them to dry thoroughly before hanging on the Christmas tree.

Above: Christmas Tree Decorations;
below left: Chocolate Truffles; below right: Nut Clusters

LUNCH FOR FRIENDS

Whether you are enjoying a break from the festivities or planning a party why not invite some friends round for lunch. Prepare the Mousse Shells, South Pacific Coffee Cake and Gammon in advance.

HONEYED GRAPEFRUIT

4 tbsp Mexican honey
4 green cardamom pods
4 fl oz/120 ml dry white wine
4 pink grapefruit
4 oz/100 g cashew nuts toasted
lime zest and slices to garnish

SERVES 4 • CALORIES PER PORTION: 318

Place honey and 4 tbsp of water in a saucepan. Remove seeds from cardamom pods, crush and add to honey. Bring to boil, stirring occasionally, reduce heat and simmer for 5 mins. Strain syrup, add wine, cover and cool. Peel grapefruit to remove pith, divide into segments. Place in individual bowls, pour cooled honey syrup over. Cover and chill for at least 1 hr. Top with cashews, garnish and serve.

MOUSSE SHELLS

2 eggs, size 3, separated
2 tbsp strawberry blossom honey
¼ pint/150 ml double cream
1 sachet powdered gelatine
6 plain chocolate shells
mint sprigs and fresh strawberries to decorate

SERVES 6 • CALORIES PER PORTION: 308

Place egg yolks and honey in a bowl and whisk until pale, thick and creamy. Lightly whip cream until just peaking, then fold into the honey mixture. Whisk egg whites until stiff, fold into mixture. Dissolve gelatine in 3 tbsp hot water and cool slightly. Fold into the mousse, ensuring it's thoroughly incorporated. Pour the mousse into a lightly greased square 7 in/18 cm cake tin. Chill for 2 hrs, or until set.

Carefully turn mousse out on to a sheet of baking parchment and, using a flower-shaped cutter, stamp out six portions, or cut mousse equally into six. Place one mousse in each chocolate shell and chill for 30 mins.

Decorate with mint and strawberries to serve.

SOUTH PACIFIC COFFEE CAKE

8 oz/225 g butter or margarine
4 oz/100 g caster sugar
4 oz/100 g South Pacific honey
4 eggs, size 3, beaten
2 tbsp coffee essence
10 oz/300 g self-raising flour
1 tsp ground ginger
1 tsp ground cinnamon
4 oz/100 g chopped mixed nuts
FOR THE FILLING:
6 oz/175 g icing sugar
3 oz/75 g butter or margarine
2 tbsp English blend set honey

CUTS INTO 24 SLICES
CALORIES PER PORTION: 245

Preheat the oven to Gas 5, 375°F, 190°C. Grease and line an 8 in/20 cm square cake tin with greased greaseproof paper. Cream fat with sugar and honey until light and fluffy. Gradually add eggs and coffee essence, beat well. Sieve flour and spices, fold into mixture with chopped nuts. Spoon mixture into tin, smooth top. Bake for 30-40 mins, then cool on a wire rack. Discard lining paper.

To make the filling, sieve 5 oz/150 g icing sugar. Cream fat and honey together until creamy then gradually beat in the icing sugar until a smooth spreadable consistency is reached. (If necessary add a little lemon juice or milk.)

Slice the cake in half horizontally, sandwich together with honey filling. Dust with remaining icing sugar and slice.

SALAD DRESSING

¼ pint/150 ml sunflower oil
2 tbsp white wine vinegar
1 garlic clove, peeled and crushed
2 tbsp freshly chopped mint
salt and freshly ground black pepper

MAKES ABOUT ½ PINT
CALORIES PER TBSP: 70

Place oil, vinegar, garlic and mint in a screw-top jar. Season with salt and pepper and shake vigorously. Use as a dressing for green salad.

GAMMON WITH APRICOT SAUCE

½ pint/300 ml red wine
5 tbsp orange blossom honey
2 bay leaves
4 lb/1.8 kg unsmoked gammon joint, boned
about 50 cloves
3 tbsp demerara sugar
15 oz/425 g can apricots in natural juice, drained
parsley sprigs to garnish

SERVES 8 • CALORIES PER PORTION: 490

Preheat the oven to Gas 4, 350°F, 180°C, 10 mins before cooking. Blend red wine with 2 tbsp honey. Add bay leaves and pour over gammon. Cover and leave in fridge for at least 6 hrs, turning occasionally.

Drain gammon, reserving the marinade. Wrap joint tightly in a double layer of foil, making a slit in top to allow steam to escape. Place in a roasting tin and cook for 1½ hrs. Remove from oven, unwrap foil, cool for 15 mins.

Increase oven temperature to Gas 7, 425°F, 220°C. Carefully strip away gammon rind. Make ⅛ in/3 mm deep cuts in fat at 1 in/2.5 cm intervals, forming a diamond

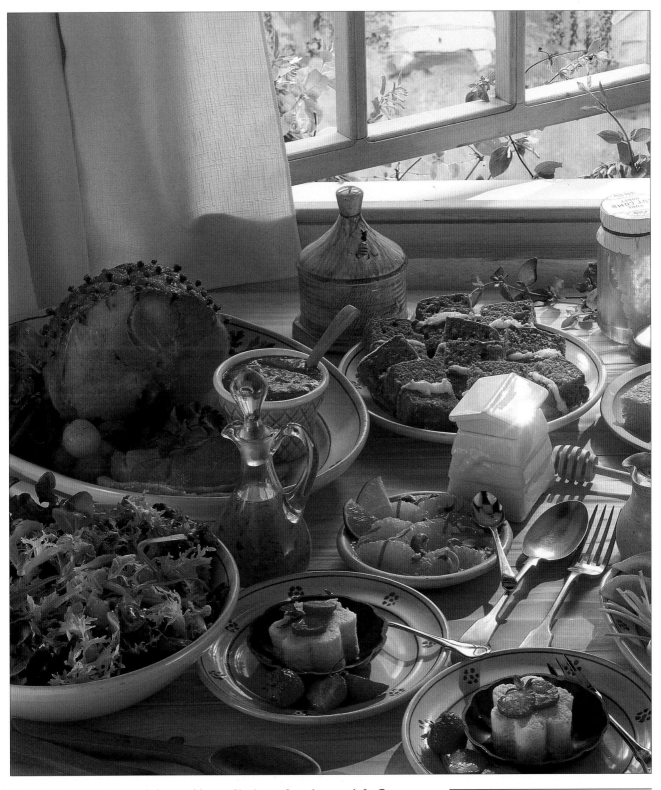

pattern. Stud each diamond shape with a clove. Spoon over remaining honey, then sprinkle with sugar. Return joint to oven, and cook for 30-40 mins. Blend apricots in a food processor with 6 tbsp of reserved marinade. Place in saucepan, bring to boil and simmer for 5 mins. Garnish gammon and serve with seasonal vegetables.

Clockwise from bottom left: Green Salad with Dressing; Gammon with Apricot Sauce; South Pacific Coffee Cake; Mousse Shells, decorated with mint sprigs and strawberries; and centre, Honeyed Grapefruit

BUFFET MEAL

Try this mouthwatering selection of recipes which are ideal for a buffet tea. There's Lamb Casserole, Monkfish Kebabs and even Fruit Tea Trifle.

MONKFISH KEBABS

1½ lb/675 g monkfish, skinned, boned, cut into 1 in/2.5 cm cubes
1 red pepper, deseeded and cubed
1 yellow pepper, deseeded and cubed
4 tomatoes, quartered
2 courgettes, trimmed and sliced
3 fl oz/85 ml fish stock
2 tbsp vegetable oil
cooked rice to serve
mint sprigs to garnish

SERVES 4 • CALORIES PER PORTION: 205

Thread the fish and vegetables on to 8 skewers. Mix the stock with the oil and brush over the kebabs. Place the kebabs under a medium hot grill and cook for 8-10 mins, turning occasionally and brushing with the stock and oil. Serve with cooked rice and garnish with mint sprigs.

LAMB CASSEROLE

3 tbsp oil
2 leeks, trimmed, washed and sliced
10 oz/300 g carrots, sliced
16 button onions, peeled
2 sticks celery, trimmed and sliced
2½ lb/1.25 kg lamb fillet cut into
    1 in/2.5 cm pieces
1½ oz/40 g cornflour
2 pints/1.2 litres chicken stock
2 tbsp tomato purée
salt and freshly ground black pepper
bay leaves to garnish

SERVES 6 • CALORIES PER PORTION: 559

Preheat the oven to Gas 4, 350°F, 180°C. Heat the oil in a large frying pan. Fry the vegetables for 2 mins then transfer to a large casserole. Fry the lamb until lightly brown, drain. Transfer to casserole. Blend the cornflour with the stock and pour into a pan. Gradually bring to the boil and simmer for 2 mins until thickened. Stir in the tomato purée and seasoning. Pour into the casserole and mix. Cover and cook in the oven for 1½ hrs or until meat is tender. Garnish with bay leaves.

STIR FRIED PRAWNS

1 tbsp sesame or vegetable oil
2 spring onions, trimmed and sliced
8 oz/227 g can bamboo shoots, drained
4 oz/100 g mangetout, trimmed
4 oz/100 g baby corn
4 oz/100 g oyster mushrooms, trimmed
1 tsp cornflour
3 fl oz/85 ml chicken stock
1 tbsp oyster sauce
2 tsp light soy sauce
freshly ground black pepper
8 oz/225 g peeled prawns, thawed if frozen
Chinese noodles to serve
spring onion tassels and whole prawns to garnish

SERVES 4 • CALORIES PER PORTION: 228

Heat the oil in a large frying pan or wok. Add the spring onions, bamboo shoots, mangetout, baby corn and mushrooms and stir fry for 2 mins. Blend the cornflour with the stock, oyster sauce, soy sauce and black pepper. Add to pan with prawns. Stir fry for a further 2 mins. Serve with Chinese noodles and garnish with spring onion tassels and whole prawns.

Note: to prepare spring onion tassels, trim the root from the bulb end and cut off the green leaves from the top leaving approx 3 in/7.5 cm in length. Make slits from the bulb end towards the leaves as finely as possible. Leave in cold water for at least 1 hr.

IMPERIAL PICKLED EGGS

¾ pint/450 ml white wine vinegar
4 garlic cloves, peeled and chopped
2 oz/50 g pickling spice
small strip of orange rind
1 blade of mace
½ pint/300 ml strong Darjeeling tea, cold
8 eggs, size 3, hard boiled and shelled

MAKES 8 • CALORIES PER PORTION: 84

Place the vinegar, garlic, pickling spice, orange rind and mace in a pan. Gradually bring to the boil, cover and simmer for 10 mins. Allow to cool then strain into a bowl. Stir in the tea. Pour a little of the tea mixture into a clean 2¼ pint/1.25 litre wide necked jar. Add the hard boiled eggs. Top up with remaining tea mixture. Seal well and label. Leave for about 4 weeks before using. For a slightly smoky flavour use Lapsang Souchong tea instead of Darjeeling.

FRUIT TEA TRIFLE

1 oz/25 g gelatine
1 pint/600 ml wild cherry tea, cold or any fruit flavoured tea of your choice
3 oz/75 g caster sugar
1 pint/600 ml sweet red wine
red food colouring (optional)
8 oz/225 g raspberries
4 oz/100 g strawberries, hulled, rinsed and sliced
4 oz/100 g seedless green grapes
1½ pint/900 ml thick ready-made custard
1¼ pint/750 ml double cream, whipped

SERVES 8 • CALORIES PER PORTION: 578

Dissolve the gelatine in 4 tbsp of the tea in a bowl over a pan of hot water. Place the remaining tea in a pan with the sugar and heat gently until all the sugar has dissolved. Allow to cool slightly then add the gelatine and wine. Stir in a few drops of red food colouring if using. Place 4 oz/100 g of the raspberries, all the strawberries and grapes in a 4 pint/2.2 litre trifle bowl. Pour over the tea mixture. Chill until set. Spoon the custard over the jelly and spread evenly with a knife. Reserve 8 tbsp of the cream. Spoon the remaining over the custard. Place the reserved cream in a piping bag and pipe around the edge of the trifle. Decorate the centre of the trifle with the reserved raspberries.

EARL GREY ICE-CREAM

¾ pint/450 ml milk
4 oz/100 g caster sugar
4 tbsp Earl Grey tea leaves
¾ pint/450 ml double cream, lightly whipped
wafer rolls to serve

SERVES 4 • CALORIES PER PORTION: 657

Set freezer to rapid freeze. Place the milk and sugar in a pan. heat gently until the sugar has dissolved. Bring to the boil, remove from heat and stir in the tea leaves. Cover and leave to infuse for 5 mins. Strain into a bowl and leave until

Clockwise from bottom left; Stir Fried Prawns; Fruit Tea Trifle; Imperial Pickled Eggs; Monkfish Kebabs; Earl Grey Ice-Cream; and Lamb Casserole

cold. Gradually fold the tea into the cream. Place in a freezable container, cover and freeze until ice crystals have started to form, about 2 hrs. Whisk the mixture until smooth, cover and freeze for about 2 hrs or until completely frozen. Remove from the freezer and leave to soften in the fridge 15 mins before serving. Serve with wafer rolls.

(Don't forget to return freezer to its normal setting once the ice cream is frozen.)

CHRISTMAS ENTERTAINING

Sauces play an essential role in the art of cooking – the right sauce can be the making of the dish and sometimes they are used to create a striking contrast to the food served.

BECHAMEL SAUCE

This is perhaps the most popular of all white sauces. The 'roux' is cooked for just 2 mins and not allowed to colour at all. Sauces that are derived from béchamel include mornay (cheese), mushroom and soubise (onion).

1 pint/600 ml milk
1 small onion
1 small carrot
1 celery stick
6 peppercorns
1 bay leaf
2 oz/50 g unsalted butter
2 oz/50 g flour
salt
2-3 tbsp cream (optional)

MAKES 1 PINT/600 ML
CALORIES PER 1 FL OZ/25 ML: 41

Place the milk in a saucepan. Peel onion, trim and peel carrot, scrub celery and trim. Place in the pan with the peppercorns and bay leaf. Bring slowly to just below boiling point, then remove from the heat. Cover and allow to infuse for at least 30 mins. Strain mixture, reserving liquid.

Melt the fat in a clean pan, stir in the flour. Cook over a gentle heat for 2 mins so that the starch grains in the flour swell and burst. Take care not to burn the roux.

Remove from heat. Strain the milk and warm slightly before using a wooden spoon to beat it into the roux. Cook the mixture over a moderate heat, stirring throughout, until the sauce thickens and coats the back of the spoon.

Add salt to taste and stir in the cream, if using. Use sauce as required.

BEARNAISE SAUCE

This sauce uses an emulsion of eggs and butter to give a thick creamy texture. The flavour is fairly sharp. Other sauces using an emulsion as a thickener include hollandaise, cucumber and mousseline (a very delicate sauce).

1 shallot, peeled and finely chopped
2 tarragon sprigs, bruised
2 chervil sprigs, bruised
2 tbsp tarragon vinegar
2 tbsp white wine vinegar
¼ pint/150 ml dry white wine
2 egg yolks, size 3
1 oz/25 g unsalted butter
salt and ground white pepper

MAKES ¼ PINT/150 ML
CALORIES PER 1 FL OZ/25 ML: 89

Place shallot, tarragon, chervil, vinegars and wine in a pan and bring to the boil. Boil vigorously until reduced by half. Strain. Place the egg yolks in the top of a double boiler or in a basin over a pan of gently simmering water, then whisk in the strained liquid. Cook, whisking throughout, until the mixture is light and fluffy.

Cut the butter into small cubes, then whisk in one piece at a time, ensuring each pieces is thoroughly incorporated before adding the next. Season to taste, then use as required.

SAUCE BERCY

1 shallot
1 oz/25 g unsalted butter
¼ pint/150 ml white wine
½ pint/300 ml chicken, fish or
   vegetable stock
salt and freshly ground black pepper
strained juice of 1 small lemon
1 tbsp freshly chopped parsley

FOR THE BEURRE MANIE:
½ oz/15 g unsalted butter
½ oz/15 g flour

MAKES 14 FL OZ/400 ML
CALORIES PER 1 FL OZ/25 ML: 42

Peel and chop the shallot, melt the butter in a pan, then sauté the shallot for 5 mins, or until softened. Add the wine, bring to the boil and boil rapidly until reduced by half. Add the stock, seasoning, lemon juice and parsley and bring back to the boil.

Beat the beurre manié ingredients together to form a paste. Drop teaspoonfuls into the pan and whisk vigorously until each is completely incorporated. Continue until all the paste has been used. Strain and use as required. For a thicker sauce, add a little more beurre manié.

ESPAGNOLE SAUCE

This is the basic brown sauce from which many other brown sauces are derived. Dripping is generally used instead of butter and the 'roux' is cooked over a very gentle heat for up to 30 mins, until it becomes golden in colour.

2 oz/50 g streaky bacon
2 oz/50 g dripping or unsalted butter
1 small onion
1 small carrot
2 oz/50 g flour
1 pint/600 ml good beef stock
2 oz/50 g mushrooms
2 tbsp tomato purée
salt and freshly ground black pepper

MAKES 14 FL OZ/400 ML
CALORIES PER 1 FL OZ/25 ML: 54

Derind bacon, discard any cartilage, then chop roughly. Heat the fat in a pan, sauté the bacon for 5 mins. Peel the onion and carrot and thinly slice. Add to the pan and cook for 5 mins. Stir in the flour, then lower the heat and cook very gently for about 20 mins, stirring occasionally, until the roux becomes golden brown. Take care not to burn it.

Stir in the stock, mushrooms and tomato purée and continue to simmer for 30 mins. If the sauce is too thick, dilute with extra beef stock. Remove from heat, strain, adjust seasoning, and use the sauce as required.

Note: sauces are best kept warm by covering with damp greaseproof paper then tin foil and placing in a bain marie and put in a moderately hot oven. This will keep most sauces warm for up to 1 hr.

PORK WITH JUNIPER BERRIES

4 x 4 oz/100 g pork escalopes
1 tbsp butter or margarine
1 tbsp oil
1 tbsp juniper berries
zested rind of 1 orange
½ pint/300 ml Sauce Bercy (see recipe on page 38)
2 tbsp soured cream
zested orange rind to garnish

SERVES 4 CALORIES PER PORTION: 524

Trim escalopes. Beat lightly with a mallet or rolling pin. Heat fat and oil in a frying pan, then fry escalopes for 2 mins on each side. Remove from pan and wipe pan with kitchen paper.

Return escalopes to pan, together with the juniper berries, orange rind and prepared Sauce Bercy. Cook over a gentle heat for 10 mins, or until thoroughly cooked. Stir in the soured cream then gently reheat. Arrange on a warm serving platter, garnish, and serve with freshly cooked vegetables.

Clockwise from bottom left: Prawn Stars; Spring Chicken Fricassée; Strawberry Tart; and, Pork with Juniper Berries

PRAWN STARS

5 large sheets of filo pastry

1 oz/25 g butter, melted

few salad leaves, washed

**4 oz/100 g peeled prawns, thawed
   if frozen**

2 tbsp mayonnaise

1 tsp tomato purée

grated rind of ½ lemon

paprika pepper to garnish

SERVES 4 • CALORIES PER PORTION: 125

Preheat the oven to Gas 6, 400°F, 200°C. Divide each pastry sheet into 3. Brush the inside of five individual star tins with a little melted butter. Place a piece of filo pastry in each tin, carefully easing into corners. Brush with melted butter and place a further sheet of pastry on top. Brush again with butter and place the final piece of pastry on top. Trim the edges and arrange tins on a baking sheet. Cook in oven for 8-10 mins until golden. Cool before removing from the tins.

Shred the salad leaves finely, then place in four of the pastry stars. Top with the peeled prawns. Place mayonnaise in a bowl and stir in the tomato purée and lemon rind, mix well. Spoon into the remaining star.

Sprinkle the prawns and mayonnaise with a little paprika pepper and serve.

SPRING CHICKEN FRICASSEE

**2 lb/900 g oven-ready free-range
   chicken**

1 lemon, halved

2 bay leaves

6 oz/175 g baby carrots

4 oz/100 g mangetout

½ small green or white cauliflower

**1 pint/600 ml Béchamel Sauce (see
   recipe on page 38)**

3 tbsp single cream

SERVES 4 • CALORIES PER PORTION: 690

Preheat the oven to Gas 5, 375°F, 190°C, 10 mins before cooking the chicken. Wash chicken inside and out, dry well. Place lemon halves and bay leaves inside the cavity. Place chicken in a roasting tin, cover with foil and cook for 1-1½ hrs, or until completely cooked and juices run clear.

Remove from oven, allow to cool, then cut off the meat from the carcass, discarding skin and bones. Cut the meat into small chunks. Cover and reserve.

Scrape and trim carrots, cook in boiling salted water for 5-8 mins, drain. Trim the mangetout and break the cauliflower into small florets. Blanch mangetout in boiling salted water for 1 min and cauliflower florets for 5 mins, then drain both.

Add the chicken and vegetables to the prepared Béchamel Sauce, stir in the cream, then spoon into a 2 pint/900 ml ovenproof dish.

Cover and place in oven for 35 mins, or until heated through and piping hot. Serve immediately.

STRAWBERRY TART

8 oz/225 g plain flour

5 oz/150 g butter or margarine

½ oz/15 g caster sugar

1 egg yolk, size 3

¾ pint/450 ml ready-made custard

8 oz/225 g fresh strawberries

3 tbsp redcurrant jelly

1 tbsp lemon juice

SERVES 8 • CALORIES PER PORTION: 401

Preheat the oven to Gas 6 400°F, 200°C, 15 mins before baking pastry case. Sieve the flour into a mixing bowl, add fat and rub in until the mixture resembles fine breadcrumbs. Stir in sugar, then add egg yolk and 2 tsp cold water. Mix to form a firm but pliable dough. Knead on a floured surface, use to line a 9 in/23 cm fluted flan case. Prick base with a fork and bake blind for 12-15 mins, or until cooked. Remove from oven and leave until cold.

When cold, fill with prepared custard and smooth the top. Hull the strawberries, wash and dry thoroughly. Cut in half and arrange over the custard.

Heat the redcurrant jelly and lemon juice together. Stir until smooth. Cool slightly then spoon over the top of the strawberries. Serve with melba sauce.

PLAICE FILLETS WITH ORANGE SAUCE

4 plaice fillets, skinned

salt and freshly ground black pepper

1 small onion

½ oz/15 g butter or margarine

2 spring onions

grated rind of ½ orange

2 oz/50 g fresh white breadcrumbs

1 oz/25 g pine nuts

2 tsp freshly chopped coriander

salt and freshly ground black pepper

1 egg yolk, size 3

¼ pint/150 ml fish stock

1 bay leaf

1 small carrot

1 celery stick

**½ pint/300 ml Béarnaise Sauce (see
   recipe on page 38)**

orange slices to garnish

**SERVES 4 AS A STARTER, 2 AS A MAIN MEAL
CALORIES PER FILLET: 459**

Preheat the oven to Gas 4, 350°F, 180°C. Trim the plaice fillets and season with salt and pepper. Cover and set aside.

Peel and finely chop the onion, melt fat in a pan, then fry onion for 5 mins, or until softened but not coloured. Remove pan from heat. Trim and chop spring onions, add to pan with orange rind, breadcrumbs, pine nuts and coriander. Season. Mix well, then bind together with the egg yolk.

Place fillets skinned side down on a chopping board. Spread the filling over fillets to within ¼ in/6 mm of edges. Roll up and secure each with a cocktail stick. Place in a shallow ovenproof dish with stock and bay leaf. Peel and slice carrot, trim and chop celery, then add to the fish. Cover and cook in oven for 10-15 mins, or until fish is cooked.

Remove from oven, drain fish and place on a warmed serving dish. Discard liquid, bay leaf and vegetables.

Pour the prepared Béarnaise Sauce over, cover again and return to oven for 5 mins, or until piping hot. Garnish with orange slices to serve.

TOURNEDOS WITH MADEIRA SAUCE

½ pint/300 ml Espagnole Sauce (see
　　recipe on page 38-39)
½ pint/300 ml beef stock
salt and freshly ground black pepper
2 fl oz/50 ml Madeira
I tbsp redcurrant jelly
4 slices of white bread
I tbsp butter
I tbsp oil
4 tournedos steaks, each approx
　　4 oz/100 g in weight
parsley sprigs to garnish

SERVES 4 • CALORIES PER PORTION: 509

Mix together the Espagnole Sauce and
stock, place in a small pan, bring to the
boil, then boil rapidly until reduced by half.
Adjust the seasoning, then add the
Madeira and redcurrant jelly. Simmer gently until smooth, then keep warm.

Cut out four 3 in/7.5 cm rounds from
the bread. Heat the butter and oil in a frying pan, then fry bread on both sides until
golden and crisp. Drain and reserve.

Trim the steaks, if necessary, then
season lightly. Place in the pan and brown
on both sides for 2 mins. Continue cooking for a further 5-8 mins, or until cooked
to personal preference. Drain. Garnish
and serve on the fried bread with the prepared sauce, creamed potatoes and salad.

POIRE BELLE HELENE

2 x 15 oz/425 g cans pear halves in
　　fruit juice
4 scoops of vanilla ice-cream
¼ pint/150 ml chocolate sauce

SERVES 4 • CALORIES PER PORTION: 445

Drain pears and arrange in four individual
sundae dishes. Place a scoop of vanilla ice-
cream on top of each, then pour a little
chocolate sauce over. Serve the remaining
sauce separately.

*Top: Tournedos with Madeira Sauce,
Middle: Plaice Fillets with Orange
Sauce, Bottom: Poire Belle Helene*

SPEEDY SNACKS

Fill them up fast with our delicious, quick snack recipes. They are super when the family is starving and you've no time to cook a meal.

THREE-DECK CROQUE

Although traditionally filled with cheese and ham, these fried sandwiches can be filled with tasty alternatives such as salami and mozzarella or cream cheese, mixed with crunchy, finely diced fruit or vegetables, such as pineapple or celery.

3 oz/75 g butter or sunflower margarine, softened
12 slices wholemeal bread, crusts removed
3 oz/75 g soft cheese with garlic and herbs
8 slices of ham, fat removed
1 tbsp oil
watercress and cherry tomatoes to garnish

SERVES 4 • CALORIES PER PORTION: 499

Using half the fat, butter one side of each bread slice. Place 4 slices, buttered side down, on a board and spread with half the soft cheese. Top with a slice of ham then a slice of bread, buttered side down. Spread with remaining cheese and ham. Finish with last 4 slices of bread, buttered side down. Butter the upper side of each sandwich and cut into halves.

Heat oil and remaining fat and fry sandwiches, carefully turning once, until golden. Drain and garnish with watercress and cherry tomatoes and serve with a selection of relishes.

Clockwise from bottom left: Pizza-in-the-Pan; Mini Kebabs; Three-deck Crôque, garnished with watercress and tomatoes; Mexican Puffs, garnished with parsley and red pepper; and Spanish-style Omelette

MINI KEBABS

16 cocktail herby pork sausages
8 oz/225 g medium-sized courgettes, trimmed and cut into chunks
8 oz/225 g mushrooms, wiped
2 tbsp redcurrant jelly
1 tbsp red wine vinegar
1 tbsp freshly chopped basil
salt and freshly ground black pepper
fresh basil to garnish

SERVES 4 • CALORIES PER PORTION: 139

Preheat grill to medium hot, just before cooking. Thread the sausages, courgette chunks and mushrooms, alternately on to four skewers. Mix together redcurrant jelly, vinegar, basil and seasoning. Brush jelly mixture over kebabs and grill for 4-5 mins, then turn, brushing again with jelly mixture. Grill for 4-5 mins, until cooked through. Serve garnished with basil on a bed of mixed rice.

MEXICAN PUFFS

As an alternative, add 4 oz/100 g thawed mixed vegetables or finely diced fresh vegetables to the rest of ingredients.

8 oz/225 g ground beef
onion salt and freshly ground black pepper
7½ oz/213 g can red kidney beans, drained and rinsed
dash of Tabasco sauce

dash of chilli sauce
I tbsp tomato purée
2 x 8 in/20 cm square sheets of frozen
   puff pastry, thawed
oil for deep frying
parsley and red pepper to garnish

SERVES 4 • CALORIES PER PORTION: 492

Place ground beef and seasoning in a frying pan and cook for 5-6 mins, stirring, until the beef is browned all over. Add kidney beans, Tabasco, chilli sauce and tomato purée. Mix well and continue to cook for 3-4 mins. Transfer to a plate and cool for 10 mins. Meanwhile, divide each pastry sheet into four squares.

Divide beef mixture between the eight pastry squares, dampen edges with water and fold over to form triangular pasties. Pinch edges to seal.

Heat the oil to 375°F, 190°C, or until a cube of bread browns in 30 secs. Add the pasties, four at a time, and fry for 4-5 mins until golden and well puffed. Drain and serve, garnished with the parsley and the red pepper.

PIZZA-IN-THE-PAN

8 oz/225 g self-raising wholemeal
   flour
salt and freshly ground black pepper
4 tbsp vegetable oil
7½ oz/213 g can chopped tomatoes,
   drained
2 tbsp tomato purée
½ tsp dried onion granules
I tbsp freshly chopped or 2 tsp dried
   oregano
6 oz/175 g mozzarella cheese, sliced
I tbsp capers
2 oz/50 g can anchovy fillets, drained
fresh oregano to garnish

SERVES 4 • CALORIES PER PORTION: 431

Preheat grill just before cooking. Sieve flour into bowl and season. Make a well and add 2 tbsp oil and 6 tbsp water, mixing to form a soft dough.

Turn on to a lightly floured surface and knead until smooth. Roll or press into a circle to fit a medium-sized frying pan, approx 9 in/23 cm in diameter.

Heat half remaining oil (1 tbsp) in the frying pan and add dough. Fry for 5-6 mins until lightly browned. Slide dough on to a plate, then turn over.

Heat remaining 1 tbsp oil in pan, then slide the dough carefully back, browned side uppermost.

Mix together chopped tomatoes, tomato purée, onion granules and oregano. Season. Spread over dough, top with cheese, and cook for a further 5 mins. Place under a medium-hot grill. Cook for 3-4 mins, until cheese melts.

Top with the capers and anchovy fillets and garnish with a little oregano.

SPANISH-STYLE OMELETTE

Try using a large leek, washed and sliced, in place of the spring onions and add 1 sliced green pepper, 2 sliced red chilli peppers, ham or spicy sausage.

2 tbsp olive oil
I garlic clove, peeled and crushed
I bunch spring onions, trimmed
   and chopped
I orange pepper, deseeded and
   chopped
2 tomatoes, sliced
5 eggs, size 3, beaten
salt and freshly ground black pepper
I tbsp freshly chopped or 2 tsp dried
   mixed herbs
2 oz/50 g stoned black olives, sliced
2 oz/50 g pimento-stuffed green
   olives, sliced
2 oz/50 g Gruyère cheese, grated
I tsp paprika

SERVES 4 • CALORIES PER PORTION: 261

Preheat grill to high. Heat oil in a large, heavy-based frying pan. Add garlic and spring onions, cook for 1-2 mins, until softened. Add pepper and tomatoes, and cook for 2 mins. Season eggs with salt and pepper, then add herbs. Pour into pan and cook until mixture is almost set. Sprinkle with olives, cheese and paprika, grill for 3 mins until golden.

Serve cut into wedges with mixed salad and crusty bread.

DELICIOUS CASSEROLES

At this time of year we're busy planning, shopping, sending cards and doing all we can to make sure we have a perfect time at Christmas. So, to make life a bit easier, here are a selection of delicious, slow-cooking casseroles and super, quick puds to give you more time for shopping!

LAMB HOT POT

Place a dish of shredded red cabbage, seasoning, a little sugar, 2 tbsp wine vinegar and ¼ pint/150 ml water in a casserole. Cook at bottom of oven. Serve with Hot Pot and fresh bread.

1½ lb/675 g lamb neck fillet, cubed
1 large onion, peeled and sliced
1 oz/25 g butter or margarine
1 oz/25 g flour
2 large carrots, peeled and sliced
½ pint/300 ml lamb stock
1 tbsp soy sauce
¼ pint/150 ml unsweetened apricot
   or orange juice
2 oz/50 g no-need-to-soak apricots,
   cut in half
1 tbsp freshly chopped parsley
salt and freshly ground black pepper
2 large potatoes, peeled and thinly
   sliced
3 tbsp oil
freshly chopped parsley to garnish

SERVES 4 • CALORIES PER PORTION: 652

Preheat oven to Gas 3, 325°F, 160°C. Fry lamb and onion in fat for 5 mins. Stir in flour, cook for 1 min. Add carrots, stock, soy sauce, fruit juice, apricots and parsley. Season. Place in 4 pint/2.25 litre oven-proof casserole dish.

Sauté potatoes in oil for 2-3 mins, drain, arrange over meat. Cover, cook for 2 hrs, or until cooked. Remove lid, cook for a further 30 mins. Garnish with chopped parsley, then serve.

PORK CASSEROLE

Boil a large pan of salted water, add tagliatelle, and by the time you've made a cup of tea, it'll be ready.

1¼ lb/550 g pork tenderloin, trimmed
   and cubed
1 onion, peeled and sliced
1 garlic clove, peeled and crushed
2 oz/50 g butter or margarine
1 red pepper, chopped
1 green pepper, chopped
2 green chilli peppers, sliced
1 oz/25 g flour
1 tsp ground coriander
1 tsp ground cumin
¾ pint/350 ml pork stock
4 tbsp crunchy peanut butter
3 tsp chilli sauce
fresh coriander sprigs to garnish

SERVES 4 • CALORIES PER PORTION: 430

Preheat oven to Gas 3, 325°F, 160°C. Fry pork, onion and garlic in fat for 5 mins, or until meat is sealed. Add peppers and continue to cook, stirring frequently for 2 mins. Stir in flour and spices and cook for a further 1 min.

Gradually blend in the stock, peanut butter chilli sauce. Season. Place in a 4 pint/2.25 litre ovenproof casserole dish, cover and cook for 2 hrs or until meat is tender.

Garnish with coriander, serve with tagliatelle.

BEEF CASSEROLE

Cook rice in the morning, drain, store covered, then quickly reheat when you get home.

1 tbsp oil
½ oz/15 g butter or margarine
1½ lb/675 g braising steak, cubed
1 onion, peeled and sliced
1 tbsp tomato purée
1 oz/25 g flour
14 oz/397 g can chopped tomatoes
14 oz/400 g can red kidney beans,
   drained and rinsed
2 tbsp freshly chopped coriander
¾ pint/450 ml beef stock
freshly cooked rice to serve
sprigs of coriander to garnish

SERVES 4 • CALORIES PER PORTION: 394

Preheat oven to Gas 3, 325°F, 160°C. Heat the oil and fat in frying pan, add beef, fry for 5-7 mins stirring meat until sealed. Add onion and tomato purée, cook for 2 mins. Stir in flour and cook for 1 min. Add tomatoes and their juice, kidney beans, freshly chopped coriander and stock. Bring to the boil, then pour into a 4 pint/2.25 litre ovenproof casserole dish. Cover and then cook in oven for 2½ hrs or until the meat is cooked. Serve with the prepared rice, garnished with sprigs of coriander.

Clockwise from bottom left: Beef Pot Roast; Pork Casserole; Liver Casserole; Lamb Hot Pot; and Beef Casserole

BEEF POT ROAST

Scrub a few large potatoes, prick with a fork, cook at bottom of oven with meat.

2 tbsp vegetable oil
3 lb/1.5 kg brisket or top rump
2 large onions, peeled and sliced
1 aubergine, trimmed and roughly chopped
2 garlic cloves, peeled and crushed
½ pint/300 ml beef stock
½ pint/300 ml red wine
salt and freshly ground black pepper
2 tbsp freshly chopped basil
8 oz/225 g tomatoes, peeled and chopped
sprigs of basil to garnish

SERVES 6 • CALORIES PER PORTION: 528

Preheat oven to Gas 3, 325°F, 160°C. Heat oil in a large flameproof casserole, fry meat until browned. Remove from pan, add vegetables, except tomatoes. Fry for 5 mins. Return meat to casserole, pour in stock and wine. Season. Add basil. Bring to just below boiling, cover. Simmer for 3 hrs, or until cooked. Add tomatoes for last 30 mins of cooking time. Garnish with basil and serve.

LIVER CASSEROLE

Peel potatoes in the morning, cut into small chunks, then they'll only take 10-12 mins to cook – you can be hiding the pressies!

1 lb/450 g ox liver, trimmed and sliced
6 oz/175 g baby onions, peeled
1 garlic clove, peeled and crushed
3 sticks celery, trimmed and sliced
2 oz/50 g butter or margarine
6 rashers back bacon, derinded and chopped
1 oz/25 g flour
1 tbsp tomato purée
½ pint/300 ml white stock
½ pint/300 ml cider
salt and freshly ground black pepper
5 fresh bay leaves

SERVES 4 • CALORIES PER PORTION: 533

Preheat oven to Gas 4, 350°F, 180°C. Cut liver slices in half. Fry onions, garlic and celery in fat for 2-3 mins. Remove from pan. Cook liver for 5 mins each side, remove, drain. Cook bacon for 3 mins each side, remove. Stir flour into pan with tomato purée. Cook for 1 min, blend in stock and cider. Place liver, onions, celery and bacon in 3 pint/7 litre ovenproof casserole dish. Pour stock over, season. Add 3 bay leaves, cover, cook for 2¼ hrs or until cooked. Garnish with bay leaves and serve.

HANDY TIPS

If preferred you can use pigs or lambs liver. If using pigs liver, proceed as above but cook for 1½ hrs. If using lambs liver, don't cut slices in half and cook for 45-55 mins.

TASTY NUT RECIPES

You don't have to be a vegetarian to enjoy the delicious taste of nuts. They contain a good proportion of protein, carbohydrates, fats and minerals – and they're versatile, too.

CHESTNUT SOUP

2 oz/50 g butter or margarine
I onion, peeled and chopped
I lb/450 g chestnuts, peeled and
   roughly chopped
2 oz/50 g plain flour
2 pint/1.2 litres vegetable or
   chicken stock
salt and freshly ground black pepper
grated rind and juice of I lemon
2 tbsp port (optional)
few drops of gravy browning
¼ pint/150 ml plain fromage frais

SERVES 6 • CALORIES PER PORTION: 265

Melt fat in a large saucepan, fry onion and chestnuts for 5 mins. Add flour, cook for 2 mins, then gradually stir in stock. Season. Bring to the boil, stirring constantly, until the soup thickens. Cover, then simmer for 30 mins, or until chestnuts are soft. Pass through a sieve or blend in a food processor until smooth. Return to pan. Stir in lemon rind and juice, port, if using, and gravy browning. Reheat gently, adjust seasoning, then stir in fromage frais. Continue to heat until hot, but not boiling, then serve.

LAMB CRESCENTS

8 oz/225 g ground lamb
I small onion, peeled and grated
grated rind of I small orange
3 oz/75 g shelled almonds, blanched
   and chopped
I tbsp freshly chopped coriander
salt and freshly ground black pepper
I egg, size 5, beaten
8 large sheets of filo pastry
2 oz/50 g butter, melted
salad leaves and cherry tomatoes
   to garnish

SERVES 6 • CALORIES PER PORTION: 258

Preheat the oven to Gas 6, 400°F, 200°C. Place the lamb and onion in a frying pan and fry gently until lamb is sealed. Remove from heat, mix in orange rind, 2 oz/50 g chopped almonds and coriander. Season to taste. Bind together with egg, then allow to cool.

Cut filo pastry into 6 in/15 cm squares. Brush one square with melted butter then place another square on top. Shape I tbsp of filling to form a small sausage. Place lengthways on to pastry square, 2 in/5 cm from one edge. Brush the edges with melted butter, then roll up, completely encasing filling. Bring the two ends round to form a crescent shape, place on a baking sheet. Repeat until all filling and pastry squares have been used (about twelve crescents).

Brush the crescents with more melted butter and sprinkle remaining almonds over. Cook for 10-15 mins, or until golden brown. Garnish and serve, hot or cold.

BACON & NUT SALAD

2 tbsp olive oil
6 oz/175 g mixed shelled nuts
grated rind of I lemon
freshly milled rock salt
12 oz/350 g young spinach leaves or
   salad leaves, washed and shaken
few leaves radicchio, washed
12 oz/350 g back bacon, trimmed
FOR THE DRESSING:
4 tbsp olive oil
2 tbsp red wine vinegar
I tbsp clear honey

SERVES 6 • CALORIES PER PORTION: 467

Preheat grill to medium 5 mins before cooking. Heat oil in a pan, add nuts and lemon rind. Cook, stirring throughout, until nuts are golden brown. Drain well, sprinkle with rock salt. Leave until cold.

Tear spinach or salad leaves and radicchio into pieces and place in salad bowl. Add nuts. Grill bacon until crispy, cut into small pieces, then add to bowl.

To make dressing, place ingredients in a small saucepan. Heat through, stirring occasionally. Pour over salad, toss well and serve immediately.

Clockwise from bottom left: delicious Basil & Mixed Nut Bake, served with tomato sauce; hot Bacon & Nut Salad; Chestnut Soup; Walnut Roulade, decorated with walnut halves, satsuma segments and mint sprig; Lamb Crescents, garnished with salad leaves and cherry tomatoes

BASIL & MIXED NUT BAKE

1½ oz/40 g butter or margarine

1 onion, peeled and chopped

1½ oz/40 g flour

½ pint/300 ml milk

6 oz/175 g shelled Brazil nuts, skinned and finely chopped or ground

2 oz/50 g shelled almonds, blanched and finely chopped or ground

2 oz/50 g shelled hazelnuts, skinned and finely chopped or ground

4 oz/100 g fresh white breadcrumbs

salt and freshly ground black pepper

3 eggs, size 3, separated

4 oz/100 g pine nuts

1 large garlic clove, peeled

2 oz/50 g fresh basil

2 oz/50 g Parmesan cheese, grated

basil sprigs to garnish

SERVES 6 • CALORIES PER PORTION: 643

Preheat the oven to Gas 4, 350°F, 180°C. Lightly grease and line the base of a 2 lb/900 g loaf tin.

Melt the fat in a saucepan then fry onion for 5 mins or until soft and transparent. Add flour and cook for a further 2 mins. Pull pan to one side then gradually stir in milk then cook, stirring throughout, until sauce thickens. Remove from heat, stir in chopped ground nuts and breadcrumbs. Season.

Whisk egg whites until stiff. Fold 2 tbsp egg white into nut mixture, then fold in the remainder. Place half this mixture into the base of the loaf tin.

Place pine nuts, garlic, basil, Parmesan and 2 egg yolks in a food processor. Add seasoning, then blend until smooth. If the mixture is very dry, add remaining egg yolk and process again. Place on top of nut mixture in the loaf tin, top with remaining nut mixture. Smooth over top, cover with foil then cook for 2 hrs, or until set and firm to the touch.

Remove from oven, leave to settle for 5 mins, then turn out on to a serving plate, discarding the lining paper. Garnish and serve with a home-made tomato sauce.

WALNUT ROULADE

3 oz/75 g shelled walnuts

3 eggs, size 3

4 oz/100 g caster sugar

3 oz/75 g self-raising flour, sieved

1 tbsp strong black coffee, cooled

7 fl oz/200 ml whipping cream

1 satsuma, peeled and segmented

2 tsp icing sugar

mint sprig to decorate

**CUTS INTO 8 SLICES
CALORIES PER PORTION: 266**

Preheat the oven to Gas 6, 400°F, 200°C. Grease and line a 12 in × 10 in/30 cm × 25 cm Swiss roll tin with greaseproof paper. Reserve a few walnut halves for decoration, then finely grind 1 oz/25 g, and finely chop the remainder.

Place the eggs and sugar in a large mixing bowl over a pan of gently simmering water. Whisk until thick and creamy, and the whisk leaves a trail when lightly pulled across the surface. Remove from heat and continue whisking until cool. Fold in the finely ground walnuts, flour and black coffee, then pour into the prepared tin. Bake in the oven for 12-15 mins, or until the cake is firm to the touch.

Invert the baked cake on to a sheet of greaseproof paper, lightly sprinkled with caster sugar. Remove tin and lining paper. Trim edges, roll up and leave until cold. Lightly whip cream until it forms soft peaks. Unroll the sponge and spread cream over to within ¼ in/6 mm of edge. Sprinkle with chopped walnuts.

Finely chop a few satsuma segments and arrange over the cream. Roll up roulade, then sieve icing sugar on top. Place on serving plate and decorate with walnut halves and mint sprig. Surround with the remaining satsuma segments.

HANDY TIP

If you have a large free-standing mixer, whisk the eggs and sugar with the balloon whisk attachment, until thick and creamy. On a high speed this will take approx 5 mins.

CANAPES

When family or friends drop by, either planned or unexpectedly, these small and tasty treats can be offered over the Christmas holiday. These delicious canapés can be prepared on the spur of the moment or well in advance.

HONEYED DOUGHNUTS

4 oz/100 g plain flour
6 oz/175 g strong plain flour
pinch of salt
½ tsp easy-blend dried yeast
1½ oz/40 g caster sugar
pinch of ground cinnamon
grated rind of ½ orange
5 fl oz/150 ml milk, warmed
1½ oz/40 g butter, melted
1 egg, size 3, beaten
oil for deep frying
4 tbsp clear honey
2 tsp lemon juice
1 oz/25 g pistachio nuts, chopped

MAKES 24 • CALORIES PER PORTION: 83

Sift the flours and salt together. Stir in the dried yeast, sugar, cinnamon and orange rind. Mix together the milk, butter and egg and pour into the flour mixture, mixing to form a smooth dough.

Turn the dough out on to a lightly floured surface and knead well for about 10 mins until smooth. Place the dough in a clean bowl, cover with a clean damp tea towel and leave in a warm place to rise for about 2 hrs or until doubled in size.

Knock the dough back and divide into 12 equal pieces. Roll into balls. Cover with a clean damp tea towel and leave in a warm place to rise for about 20 mins, or until doubled in size.

Heat the oil for deep frying to 180°C, 350°F. Place 5 or 6 doughnuts in the oil and fry for 2 mins, turning once, or until golden brown. Drain on kitchen paper. Repeat until all the doughnuts are cooked.

Heat the honey and lemon juice in a saucepan until melted. Dip the doughnuts into the honey to coat completely. Place on a cooling rack with greaseproof paper underneath. Sprinkle the pistachio nuts over the top of the doughnuts and leave to cool. Place in paper cases and serve.

MINI CHOCOLATE ECLAIRS

2½ oz/65 g strong plain white flour
2 oz/50 g butter
2 eggs, size 3, beaten
2 oz/50 g plain chocolate, broken into pieces
3 fl oz/85 ml double cream

MAKES 24 • CALORIES PER ECLAIR: 61

Preheat the oven to Gas 6, 400°F, 200°C, 15 mins before cooking pastry.

Sieve the flour on to a sheet of greaseproof paper. Place the butter in a saucepan with ¼ pint/150 ml water, bring to the boil until the fat has melted. Remove the pan from the heat and add all the flour at once. Beat well until fully incorporated and the mixture forms a ball. Add the eggs a little at a time, beating well after each addition bringing the mixture back to its original consistency before adding any more egg. The mixture should become smooth and glossy.

Place mixture in a piping bag fitted with a ½ in/1.25 cm plain nozzle. Lightly grease two baking sheets and pipe 48 × 1.5 in/4 cm lengths on to the tray. Place in the oven and cook for 15 mins or until risen and golden. Remove from the oven. Place on a cooling rack until completely cold.

Melt the chocolate in a bowl over a pan of water and spoon over the top of 24 eclairs. Leave to set.

Meanwhile whip the cream until it peaks, pipe onto the remaining eclairs. Sandwich together with the chocolate topped eclair. Chill until required.

FRUIT CUSTARD TARTS

FOR THE PASTRY:
5 oz/150 g plain flour
pinch of salt
1 tsp caster sugar
3 oz/75 g butter
1 egg, size 3, beaten
FOR THE CREME PATISSIERE:
2 eggs, size 3, beaten
2 oz/50 g caster sugar
2 tbsp cornflour
2 tbsp flour
½ pint/300 ml milk
few drops of vanilla essence
1 kiwi fruit, peeled and sliced
4 oz/100 g raspberries, thawed if frozen
mint sprigs to decorate

MAKES 24 • CALORIES PER TART: 62

Preheat the oven to Gas 6, 400°F, 200°C. Sift the flour and salt into a bowl. Stir in the

Clockwise from top left: Mini Chocolate Eclairs; Fruit Custard Tarts; Honeyed Doughnuts; Smoked Chicken Croûtes; Scrambled Egg Blinis; Smoked Salmon Blinis; Taramasalata Croûtes

sugar. Cut the butter into cubes and rub into the flour and sugar. Make a well in the centre and stir in the egg. Bring together with your fingers to form a dough. Wrap and chill for 30 mins.

Meanwhile make the crème patissière. Cream the eggs and sugar together until thick and pale. Sift the cornflour and flour into a bowl and beat in a little of the milk to form a paste, then beat into the egg mixture. Heat the remaining milk until almost boiling and pour over the egg mixture. Strain the mixture into a clean saucepan. Bring the mixture to the boil, stirring continuously. Add the vanilla essence and cook for a further 2 mins. Remove from heat and allow to cool.

Roll out the pastry on a lightly floured surface. Use to line twenty-four 2 in/5 cm flan tins. Prick the base with a fork. Place on a baking sheet and bake blind for 5 mins. Remove baking beans and cook for a further 7 mins. Remove from tins and allow to cool completely.

Once cool, half fill the pastry cases with the prepared crème patissière. Arrange the fruit on top and decorate with mint just before serving.

SMOKED CHICKEN CROUTES

3 slices white medium sliced bread
1 tbsp olive oil
1 tbsp butter
6 oz/175 g smoked chicken
4 tbsp cranberry sauce
flat leaf parsley to garnish

MAKES 24 • CALORIES PER CROUTE: 38

Remove the crusts from the bread and cut each slice into eight triangles. Heat the oil and butter in a frying pan and fry the bread for 5 mins, turning once, until golden brown. Drain well.

Slice the chicken into small, thin strips and arrange on the fried croûtes. Spoon the cranberry sauce over the chicken, garnish and serve.

SMOKED SALMON BLINIS

2 tsp fresh yeast
8 fl oz/250 ml milk, warmed
2½ oz/65 g flour
1 tsp caster sugar
pinch of salt
1 tbsp butter, melted
1 egg separated
1 tbsp olive oil
4 oz/100 g smoked salmon
6 oz/175 g full fat cream cheese
lemon butterflies and dill sprigs to garnish

SERVES 24 • CALORIES PER BLINI: 66

Dissolve the yeast in 2 fl oz/50 ml of the milk. Add 1 tbsp flour and place the mixture in a warm place until doubled in volume. Add the remaining tepid milk, the flour, sugar, salt, melted butter and the egg yolk. Beat to a smooth batter. Place in a warm place until doubled in volume. Beat lightly and leave to rise until doubled in size again. Add the whisked egg white and heat 1 tbsp of oil in a frying pan. Spoon small amounts of the mixture into the pan and cook for 3-4 mins each side.

Use a 2 in/5 cm heart cutter and cut four shapes from each blini.

Meanwhile cut the smoked salmon into thin strips and spread with the cheese. Roll up and cut into rounds. Place a round on to each of the blinis and garnish. Serve.

SCRAMBLED EGG BLINIS

2 tsp fresh yeast
8 fl oz/250 ml milk, warmed
2½ oz/65 g flour
1 tsp caster sugar
pinch of salt
1 tbsp butter, melted
1 egg, separated
1 tbsp oil
1 oz/25 g butter
4 eggs, beaten
4 tbsp milk
salt and freshly ground black pepper
1 tbsp chopped chives
chives to garnish

MAKES 24 • CALORIES PER BLINI: 45

Make the blinis as for the previous recipe. Use a small petal-shaped cutter to cut out 24 shapes.

Melt the butter in a saucepan and add the beaten eggs, milk, seasoning and chopped chives. Cook the egg mixture gently until lightly scrambled, stirring frequently. Transfer to the blini shapes, garnish and serve.

TARAMASALATA CROUTES

3 slices medium sliced white bread
1 tbsp olive oil
3 oz/75 g taramasalata
lime butterflies, chervil and mixed peppercorns to garnish

MAKES 24 • CALORIES PER CROUTE: 24

Remove crusts from the bread and cut out 24 x 1¼ in/4.6 cm circles. Heat the oil in a frying pan and fry for 5 mins, turning until golden. Drain well.

Place the taramasalata in a piping bag fitted with a star nozzle and pipe on to croûtes. Garnish and serve.

CHRISTMAS DRINKS & NIBBLES

We've got something to suit everyone...delicious, non-alcoholic punches, for the kids and drivers, warming drinks with a touch of spirit, plus some tasty nibbles – both sweet and savoury – that your friends and family are sure to love.

Clockwise from bottom left: Sesame Brazils; smooth, warming Coffee Cup; Two-Colour Chocolate Crisps; refreshing Lemon Sweet & Sour; fruity Cranberry Crush; crunchy Spicy Mix; Pernod & Orange Crush; and Grape Punch

SPICY MIX

2 tbsp vegetable oil
4 oz/100 g unsalted cashew nuts
2 oz/50 g whole blanched almonds
2 oz/50 g pretzel sticks, broken into
    2 in/5 cm lengths
2 tsp turmeric
½ tsp ground coriander
½ tsp ground cumin
1 tsp salt
2 oz/50 g small spicy cooked
    poppadums, broken into pieces

SERVES 6 • CALORIES PER PORTION: 272

Heat the oil in a heavy-based frying pan. Add the cashew nuts, almonds and pretzel sticks. Cook, stirring constantly, for 2-3 mins. Add the spices and salt, then cook for a further 1-2 mins, mixing well. Remove from heat and gently fold in poppadums. Drain and leave to cool before serving.

SESAME BRAZILS

1 lb/450 g Brazil nuts, shelled
8 oz/225 g caster sugar
oil for deep-frying
4 tbsp sesame seeds

SERVES 6 • CALORIES PER PORTION: 404

Place the nuts in boiling water and leave to soak for 10 mins. Drain, then remove skin from nuts. Place the caster sugar in a saucepan with ¾ pint/450 ml water and heat gently until the sugar dissolves. Add nuts to the syrup and bring to the boil. Boil rapidly for 10 mins, remove from the heat, cover and stand for 2 hrs.

Heat the oil in a wok or a deep-fryer until it reaches smoking point. Using a slotted spoon, remove the nuts from the syrup and cook in the oil for 2-3 mins. Drain well. Place the sesame seeds in a dish, add the nuts and toss well to coat. Leave to cool before serving.

TWO-COLOUR CHOCOLATE CRISPS

10 oz/300 g plain chocolate
10 oz/300 g white chocolate
6 oz/175 g unsalted crisps

SERVES 6 • CALORIES PER PORTION: 658

Break the plain chocolate and white chocolate into two separate bowls. Place each bowl over a saucepan of hot water, ensuring the water does not touch the base of the bowl. Heat until the chocolate has melted. Using tongs, dip crisps into the chocolate, coating well. Place on vegetable parchment paper until set.

CRANBERRY CRUSH

1½ pint/900 ml cranberry juice
½ pint/300 ml lemonade
3 fl oz/85 ml raspberry cordial
1 tbsp cloves

SERVES 6 • CALORIES PER PORTION: 123

Place all the ingredients in a saucepan over a medium heat. Heat for 20 mins, then serve.

COFFEE CUP

¼ pint/150 ml coffee liqueur, such as
    Tia Maria
1 pint/600 ml freshly made medium-
    strength black coffee
2 tbsp muscovado sugar
¼ pint/150 ml whipping cream
12 chocolate coffee beans (optional)

SERVES 6 • CALORIES PER PORTION: 172

Place the coffee liqueur, black coffee and muscovado sugar in a large saucepan.

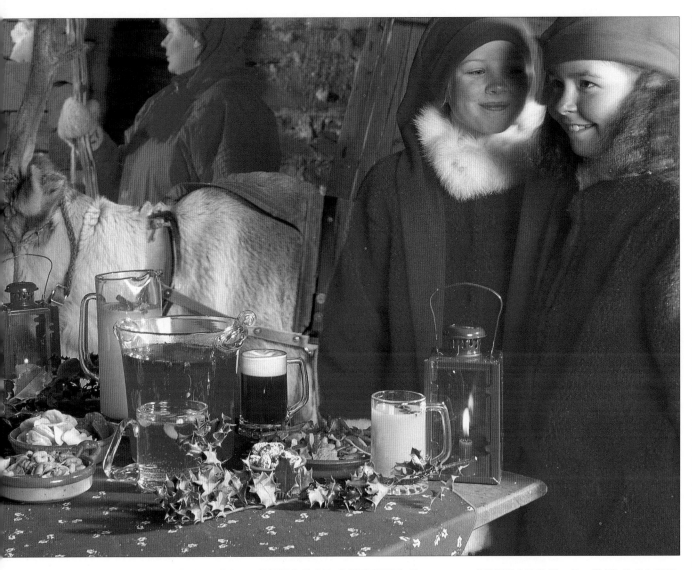

Warm over a gentle heat and stir until the sugar has dissolved. Pour into six glass tankards.

Whip the cream until softly peaking. Spoon on to the hot coffee mixture and top with coffee beans, if using.

GRAPE PUNCH

1 pint/600 ml white grape juice
½ pint/300 ml apple juice
1 tbsp caster sugar
6 cloves
2 oz/50 g seedless green grapes

SERVES 6 • CALORIES PER PORTION: 84

Place all the ingredients, except the grapes, in a large pan over a medium heat for 20 mins. Add grapes and heat for a further 5 mins. Remove the cloves and serve immediately.

LEMON SWEET & SOUR

¼ pint/150 ml gin
4 tbsp clear honey
1½ pint/900 ml lemon crush
1 cinnamon stick, lightly bruised
lemon slices and cinnamon stick to decorate

SERVES 6 • CALORIES PER PORTION: 77

Place the gin, honey, lemon crush and cinnamon stick in a large saucepan over a medium heat for 20 mins. Strain mixture, discard the bruised cinnamon stick and serve hot, decorated with lemon slices and the cinnamon stick.

PERNOD & ORANGE PUNCH

¼ pint/150 ml Pernod
½ pint/300 ml unsweetened orange juice
8 pieces of star anise
pared rind of 1 orange
6 tbsp Cointreau

SERVES 6 • CALORIES PER PORTION: 118

Place the Pernod, strained orange juice, ¾ pint/450 ml water, star anise and the pared orange rind in a large saucepan. Bring to the boil, stirring well. Reduce the heat and simmer for 20 mins. Remove from the heat then stir in the Cointreau and serve hot.

VICTORIAN CHRISTMAS EVE

On the night before Christmas, lay on this mouthwatering spread to get everyone in the party spirit. There's succulent ham, savoury strudel and fruity mince pies.

WINTER SALAD

I head frisée lettuce, washed
I carton mustard and cress, washed and trimmed
4 small cooked beetroot, sliced
4 eggs, size 3, hard-boiled, shelled and quartered
I small fennel bulb, trimmed and finely sliced
few parsley sprigs, washed
3 tbsp olive oil
I tbsp white wine vinegar
salt and freshly ground black pepper

SERVES 8 • CALORIES PER PORTION: 97

Break lettuce into small shreds and arrange on a serving platter. Add cress, beetroot, eggs, fennel and parsley. Toss gently. Mix together the oil, vinegar and seasoning. Pour over salad to serve.

TOMATO STRUDEL

2 tsp sunflower oil
I onion, peeled and chopped
14 oz/397 g can chopped tomatoes
I tbsp freshly chopped thyme
6 oz/175 g chopped mixed nuts
4 oz/100 g fresh white breadcrumbs
4 tbsp grated Parmesan cheese
salt and freshly ground black pepper
10 oz/300 g pack filo pastry sheets, thawed if frozen
2 oz/50 g butter or sunflower margarine, melted
thyme sprigs to garnish

SERVES 8 • CALORIES PER PORTION: 333

Preheat the oven to Gas 5, 375°F, 190°C, 10 mins before baking. Heat oil in a pan and sauté onion for 2-3 mins. Add tomatoes, thyme and nuts and cook for a further 5 mins. Remove from heat. Stir in the breadcrumbs and Parmesan cheese.

Season to taste. Allow to cool.

Reserving two sheets, brush filo with melted fat and overlap to form a rectangle 14 in × 20 in/36 cm × 51 cm. Spread tomato mixture over pastry, leaving 1 in/2.5 cm space round edges. Fold over edges and secure with melted fat, then carefully roll up from widest side to form a roll. Transfer to greased baking sheet and brush with melted fat. Using a leaf-shaped cutter, stamp out shapes from reserved filo and arrange over strudel, securing with melted fat. Bake for 25-30 mins or until golden. Serve hot or cold, garnished with thyme, on a bed of salad.

COLD BOILED HAM

8 lb/3.5 kg ham on the bone
2 tbsp white wine vinegar
2 celery sticks, washed
I carrot, scrubbed
I onion, peeled and studded with 5 cloves
2 bay leaves
2 tbsp light brown sugar
3 oz/75 g dried breadcrumbs
bay leaves to garnish

SERVES 8 • CALORIES PER PORTION: 390

Soak ham overnight in vinegar and enough water to cover. Rinse thoroughly. Place in a large saucepan with celery, carrot, onion, bay leaves and sugar. Cover with water. Bring to boil and remove scum.

Reduce heat, cover and, keeping water at a simmer, cook for 20 mins per lb/450 g plus 20 mins, until tender. (Remove scum that appears.) Leave the gammon to cool in the liquid then drain and strip off skin. Cover with breadcrumbs and place paper ruffle round knuckle bone. Serve garnished with bay leaves.

Any ham that's left will make a tasty treat for tea!

CITRUS MINCE PIES

10 oz/300 g plain flour
pinch of salt
8 oz/225 g butter or margarine, chilled
1½ tbsp caster sugar
I tsp finely grated orange rind
I tsp finely grated lemon rind
I egg yolk, size 3
1-2 tbsp mixed orange and lemon juice
I lb/450 g mincemeat
2-3 tbsp brandy (optional)
icing sugar to dust

MAKES 16 • CALORIES PER PIE: 248

Preheat the oven to Gas 5, 375°F, 190°C, 10 mins before baking. Sieve flour and salt into bowl. Rub in fat until mixture resembles fine breadcrumbs, stir in sugar and rinds. Bind together with egg yolk and enough juice to form a firm dough. Wrap and chill for 30 mins.

Roll out pastry thinly on a lightly floured surface. Next, using a plain round 3 in/ 7.5 cm cutter, stamp out 16 circles and use to line lightly greased bun tins. Then, using a 2 in/5 cm cutter, stamp out sixteen circles and from each cut a ½ in/1.25 cm round from the centre.

Fill cases with mincemeat, dampen edges and place smaller circles on top. Bake for 20-25 mins. Cool slightly before transferring to a wire rack. Using a small funnel pour brandy (if using) into central hole of each pie, and dust with icing sugar. Serve hot or cold.

Clockwise from top left: Citrus Mince Pies; Cold Boiled Ham, garnished with bay leaves; Mulled Wine; Crystal Fruits; Tomato Strudel; Chocolate Creams with Crystal Fruits; centre, Winter Salad

CHOCOLATE CREAMS & CRYSTAL FRUITS

8 oz/225 g plain chocolate

1 oz/25 g caster sugar

2 tbsp brandy or orange juice

1 pint/600 ml double cream

1 egg white, size 3

1 lb/450 g selection of small fruits, such as red and white grapes, Cape gooseberries and strawberries

4 oz/100 g caster sugar

mint sprigs to decorate

SERVES 8 • CALORIES PER PORTION: 517

Melt chocolate in a bowl over a pan of simmering water stirring occasionally. Cool for 10 mins then stir in sugar and brandy or orange juice. Whisk in cream, a little at a time, until forming a peak. Chill for 1 hr.

Meanwhile lightly beat the egg white, brush over lightly rinsed and dried fruits and then dip in sugar. Dry on wire rack.

Fill a large piping bag fitted with a star nozzle with chocolate cream and pipe on to individual serving dishes. Decorate with mint and serve with Crystal Fruits.

MULLED WINE

½ tsp ground ginger

6 cloves

1 cinnamon stick, bruised

pinch of grated nutmeg

6 oz/175 g caster sugar

1 orange, washed and sliced

1 pint/600 ml red wine, such as claret

SERVES 8 • CALORIES PER PORTION: 141

Place spices, sugar and half the orange in a pan with ½ pint/300 ml water. Bring to the boil, remove from heat and cool for at least 1 hr. Just before serving, add wine and heat gently. Strain and serve hot with remaining orange slices.

HANDY TIPS

Planning ahead will make the countdown to Christmas so much easier and you'll feel more relaxed on the day.

Two to Three days before:
• Thaw the turkey.
• If you haven't made one by now, buy a Christmas pudding to save time.
• Make mince pies. Warm through before serving.
• Make stuffing and leave covered in fridge.
• Stuff turkey with stuffing. Leave overnight in fridge.
• Prepare root vegetables, leave covered with cold water.
• Prepare green vegetables and salad ingredients. Leave in polythene bags in fridge.
Prepare Brandy Butter.
Lay table for Christmas lunch.

FINNISH-STYLE CHRISTMAS EVE

This Scandinavian-style menu offers a charming alternative to traditional Christmas Eve fare. It also makes an unusual New Year's Eve dinner.

MIXED FRUIT SOUP

I lb/450 g mixed dried fruit
2 oz/50 g soft light brown sugar
I cinnamon stick, lightly bruised
½ tsp grated nutmeg
8 whole cloves
2 tbsp cornflour

SERVES 10 • CALORIES PER PORTION: 104

Place dried fruit in a large bowl. Sprinkle with I oz/25 g sugar. Pour 4 pints/2.25 litres cold water over, cover, leave over-night.

Transfer fruit and water to a large saucepan. Add cinnamon stick, nutmeg and cloves. Bring to boil, reduce heat and simmer for 15-20 mins, or until the fruit has softened. Remove fruit from pan and place in a 4 pint/2.25 litre soup tureen. Discard cinnamon stick and cloves.

Blend the cornflour with 8 tbsp cold water and stir into fruit liquid until thickened. Pour thickened juices into the tureen and sprinkle with the remaining sugar to serve.

ROLL-MOP HERRINGS

10 herrings, cleaned and filleted
½ pint/300 ml dill vinegar
3 oz/75 g caster sugar
4 red onions, peeled and sliced
2 tbsp lemon juice
3 carrots, peeled and sliced
20 mixed-coloured peppercorns
I tsp mustard seeds
6 bay leaves
dill sprigs to garnish

SERVES 10 • CALORIES PER PORTION: 120

Cut herrings in half, then roll up from head end and secure with a cocktail stick. Place in a shallow dish and immerse completely in water. Cover, leave in fridge overnight.

Place vinegar and sugar in a pan with I pint/600 ml water. Boil for 3 mins, then allow to cool. Remove herrings from water and place in a shallow serving dish. Add the onions, lemon juice, carrots, peppercorns, mustard seeds and bay leaves. Pour cooled vinegar over fish, cover and marinate in fridge for up to 4 days. Garnish and serve with rye bread.

LIVER & BRANDY PATE

1¼ lb/550 g lamb's liver, trimmed and washed
3 oz/75 g smoked back bacon, rind removed
4 oz/100 g fresh white breadcrumbs
½ pint/300 ml double cream
I oz/25 g butter or margarine
I onion, peeled and chopped
¼ pint/150 ml brandy
3 eggs, size 3, beaten
salt and freshly ground black pepper
fresh herbs, mustard seeds and
    slivers of carrot
I tsp powdered gelatine
¼ pint/150 ml chicken stock
mixed salad leaves to garnish

SERVES 10 • CALORIES PER PORTION: 362

Preheat the oven to Gas 4, 350°F, 180°C. Lightly grease ten ¼ pint/150 ml individual loaf tins. Finely mince liver and bacon. Mix breadcrumbs and cream in a bowl, let stand for 10 mins, or until bread has swollen.

Melt fat in a frying pan and sauté onion for 5 mins. Drain and blend in a food processor with the breadcrumb mixture, brandy and eggs for 2 mins, or until mixture is smooth. Season. Stir in meat. Place in prepared tins, cover with foil and place in roasting tin with enough hot water to reach halfway up sides of pâté tins. Cook for 35-40 mins, or until pâté begins to shrink away from the sides of the tin.

Remove pâté tins from roasting tin, leave to cool. Arrange herbs, mustard seeds and carrot on top of pâtés. Dissolve gelatine in stock, then pour over pâté to form a ¼ in/6 mm layer. Leave until set. Remove pâté from tins, garnish and serve with crackers.

RED CABBAGE SALAD

1½ lb/675 g red cabbage
I lb/450 g jar blackcurrant jelly
FOR THE DRESSING:
2 tbsp vegetable oil
2 tbsp raspberry vinegar
I tsp wholegrain mustard
pinch of salt

SERVES 10 • CALORIES PER PORTION: 158

Trim outer leaves and base from cabbage. Discard. Halve, core and finely shred the cabbage, then wash and drain thoroughly. Lightly warm the blackcurrant jelly, stir until smooth, then place in a salad bowl together with the shredded red cabbage.

Place dressing ingredients in a clean, screw-top jar and shake vigorously. Pour dressing over the salad and toss well.

POTATO CASSEROLE

6 lb/2.75 kg potatoes, peeled and roughly chopped
5 oz/150 g butter or margarine
salt and freshly ground black pepper
1 oz/25 g flour
6 fl oz/175 ml milk, warmed
¼ pint/150 ml soured cream
1 tsp freshly grated nutmeg
2 leeks, trimmed, thinly sliced, blanched and drained
4 oz/100 g stale white breadcrumbs

SERVES 10 • CALORIES PER PORTION: 383

Preheat the oven to Gas 5, 375°F, 190°C, 10 mins before cooking. Place potatoes in a pan of boiling water and cook for 15-20 mins. Drain, then mash with 4 oz/100 g fat. Season and stir in ½ oz/15 g flour. Sprinkle remaining flour over potato, cover and leave to stand overnight.

Stir in milk and soured cream, then beat until mixture forms a smooth paste. Adjust seasoning, then add nutmeg and blanched leeks. Place in a 4 pint/2.25 litre casserole. Sprinkle breadcrumbs over top of potato and dot with remaining butter. Bake for 40 mins, or until crisp and golden.

APPLE-BAKED HAM

6 lb/2.75 kg unsmoked bacon joint
1 pint/600 ml apple juice
1 cinnamon stick, bruised
2-3 tbsp soft light brown sugar
2-3 tbsp stale white breadcrumbs
26-30 cloves
1-2 tbsp dried mustard
apple slices and salad to garnish

SERVES 10 • CALORIES PER PORTION: 693

Preheat the oven to Gas 5, 375°F, 190°C. Rinse bacon under cold running water, then pat dry with kitchen paper. Place on a trivet in a roasting tin and pour apple juice over. Add cinnamon stick, cover with foil, cook in oven for 1¾-2 hrs, or until cooked.

Remove ham from oven. Cut away skin and any underlying fat. Mix together the sugar and breadcrumbs, then spread over ham. Stud surface with cloves, reserving a few for garnishing sauce. Cook, uncovered, for 10-20 mins, or until coating is crisp. Place ham on a serving dish. Stir mustard into pan juices, then serve as a sauce with the ham. Garnish.

If liked, thicken juices by adding 1½ tbsp cornflour.

CRANBERRY MOUSSE

6 oz/175 g caster sugar
1 lb/450 g cranberries, thawed if frozen
juice of 1 lemon
juice of 1 orange
5 tsp gelatine
1 pint/600 ml double cream

SERVES 10 • CALORIES PER PORTION: 334

Place sugar in a heavy-based pan with 1 pint/600 ml water. Heat gently until sugar dissolves, then boil rapidly for 5 mins. Reduce heat, then add cranberries to syrup, reserving a few for decoration. Cook for 10-15 mins, or until cranberries have popped and are soft and mushy. Remove from heat and add fruit juices. Cool slightly, then blend in a food processor to form a purée. Dissolve the gelatine in 5 tbsp hot water, then stir into cranberries. Place in a large bowl and cool.

Whip cream until softly peaking, then fold into cranberries. Mix well. Pour into a 2½ pint/1.5 litre mould and chill until set. Turn out and decorate with reserved berries. Serve with sweet biscuits.

Clockwise from bottom left: delicious Cranberry Mousse, served with sweet biscuits; rye bread; tasty Potato Casserole; crunchy Red Cabbage Salad; mouthwatering Apple-baked Ham, served with a spicy apple sauce; winter-warming Mixed Fruit Soup; Liver & Brandy Pâté, garnished with salad leaves; and, centre, Roll-mop Herrings

VICTORIAN CHRISTMAS DAY

Everyone dreams of a terrific turkey, tasty stuffing and perfect vegetables...so, follow our simple recipes for a super special meal – and make their Big Day!

MIXED FISH PLATTER

1 lollo rosso lettuce, washed and
   dried
8 oz/225 g smoked mackerel fillets
   with black peppercorns, skinned
8 oz/225 g kipper fillets, skinned
6 oz/175 g rollmop herrings, drained
1 small red onion, peeled and sliced
1 tbsp pink peppercorns in brine,
   drained
2 tbsp red wine vinegar
1 tbsp clear honey
dill sprigs to garnish

SERVES 8 • CALORIES PER PORTION: 144

Break up the lettuce into small pieces and arrange on a serving plate. Slice mackerel and kipper into bite-sized pieces and arrange on lettuce together with rollmops. Top with onion and peppercorns. Chill until needed.

To serve, mix together the vinegar and honey and pour over salad. Garnish. Serve with lemon wedges and rye bread.

CRANBERRY & ORANGE STUFFING

8 oz/225 g cranberries, thawed if
   frozen
2 tbsp clear honey
2 oz/50 g butter or margarine
1 small onion, peeled and chopped
8 oz/225 g fresh white breadcrumbs
finely grated rind and juice of
   1 orange
2 eggs, size 3, beaten
2 tsp mixed herbs
salt and freshly ground black pepper

SERVES 8 • CALORIES PER PORTION: 137

Place the cranberries in a pan with the clear honey and ¼ pint/150 ml water. Bring to the boil, simmer for 10 mins until just softened. Drain and discard any remaining liquid.

Melt fat in pan and sauté onion for 2-3 mins, or until softened. Stir in the cranberries, breadcrumbs, orange rind and juice, eggs and herbs. Season. Mix well and use to stuff the turkey and make the stuffing balls.

ROAST TURKEY

10 lb/4.5 kg oven-ready turkey, with
   giblets, thawed if frozen
2 onions, peeled
1 orange, halved
Cranberry & Orange Stuffing
   (see recipe)
1 oz/25 g butter or margarine
2 tbsp sunflower oil
1 carrot, scrubbed
2 bay leaves
2 sticks celery
8 black peppercorns
fresh herbs and orange slices to
   garnish

SERVES 8 • CALORIES PER PORTION: 483

Preheat the oven to Gas 4, 350°F, 180°C. Remove giblets and reserve, wash and dry turkey inside and out. Place 1 onion and orange halves in body cavity. Stuff neck end with half of the stuffing and secure with a skewer, then spread whole turkey with fat. Weigh the stuffed turkey and calculate cooking time: 20 mins per lb/450 g, plus an extra 20 mins. Place turkey on a trivet in a large roasting tin, cover with foil and bake for calculated time. Remove foil 30 mins before end of the cooking time.

Form remaining stuffing into walnut-sized balls and place in a small tin. Spoon oil over, and place in oven 30 mins before turkey is cooked. The turkey juices will run clear when bird is fully cooked.

Wash giblets and place in pan with remaining onion, carrot, bay leaves, celery, peppercorns and 2 pints/2 litres cold water. Bring to boil, simmer for 45 mins. Strain and use for Turkey Gravy.

Garnish turkey and serve with stuffing balls and a cranberry sauce of your choice.

Remember to check your oven manufacturer's guide for their recommended turkey cooking temperatures as different ovens can vary. Also allow for lower power levels on Christmas Day.

TURKEY GRAVY

6 tbsp turkey juices from tin
2 oz/50 g plain flour
1½ pint/900 ml giblet stock
few drops gravy browning
salt and freshly ground black pepper

MAKES ¾ PINT/1 LITRE
CALORIES PER FL OZ/25 ML: 14

Heat the turkey juices in a pan. Stir in the flour and cook for 1-2 mins. Remove from the heat and gradually stir in stock and gravy browning. Season. Cook for 2-3 mins, stirring until thickened.

BREAD SAUCE

1 pint/600 ml milk
1 onion, peeled and studded with
   4 cloves
2 bay leaves
pinch of grated nutmeg
pinch of ground mace
6 oz/175 g stale white breadcrumbs
2 oz/50 g butter or margarine
salt and freshly ground black pepper
bay leaves to garnish

SERVES 8 • CALORIES PER PORTION: 149

Place milk, onion, bay leaves, nutmeg and mace in a pan. Bring to the boil, cover and

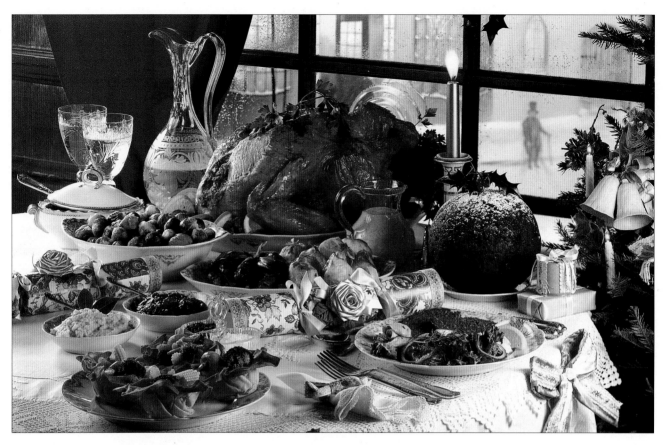

Clockwise from top left: Brussels; Gravy; Roast Turkey; cream; pud; Fish Platter; Veg Baskets; Bread Sauce; centre, Sausage Parcels and Garlic Roasties

simmer for 30 mins. Remove from heat, cool. Strain, return to a clean pan and stir in breadcrumbs, fat and seasoning. Cook over a low heat for 15 mins, stirring occasionally, until thick. Garnish to serve.

GARLIC ROASTIES

3 lb/1.5 kg medium-sized potatoes, peeled and halved
5 tbsp sunflower oil
2 garlic cloves, peeled and sliced
parsley sprigs to garnish

SERVES 8 • CALORIES PER PORTION: 219

Preheat the oven to Gas 4, 350°F, 180°C. Parboil potatoes for 5 mins. Drain. Heat oil in tin in oven for 3-4 mins, add potatoes and garlic and cook for 1 hr, basting occasionally. Increase the oven temp to Gas 7, 425°F, 220°C, and cook for a further 15 mins after turkey comes out of oven. Drain, garnish with parsley and serve.

SAUSAGE PARCELS

24 large basil leaves, washed
24 cocktail sausages
6 oz/175 g Parma ham, cut into thin strips
basil to garnish

SERVES 8 • CALORIES PER PORTION: 138

Preheat the oven to Gas 4, 350°F, 180°C. Wrap a basil leaf around each sausage, and then a strip of Parma ham. Place in a small roasting pan and bake for 25-30 mins until golden. Garnish to serve.

BRUSSELS WITH CHESTNUTS

2 lb/900 g Brussels sprouts
1 oz/25 g butter or margarine
12 oz/350 g can chestnuts, drained
salt and freshly ground black pepper

SERVES 8 • CALORIES PER PORTION: 138

Trim base from sprouts and discard outer leaves. Cut a small cross in base of each sprout and place in pan of lightly salted boiling water to cook for 10-12 mins until

tender. Meanwhile, melt the fat and sauté the chestnuts for 4-5 mins until heated through. Drain sprouts and add to the chestnuts. Mix well, season and serve.

BABY VEG BASKETS

3 oz/75 g butter or margarine
32 x 7 in/18 cm squares filo pastry
12 oz/350 g mixed baby vegetables, such as corn, carrots,
turnips and broccoli, washed and trimmed

SERVES 8 • CALORIES PER PORTION: 183

Preheat the oven to Gas 7, 425°F, 220°C. Melt fat, brush over each pastry square. Sandwich in pairs. Line eight deep muffin tins with half sandwiched filo, brush with fat and press remaining filo on top at an angle so that layers form a star shape, giving a fluted basket effect. Brush with fat, bake for 5-6 mins. Meanwhile, dice corn and carrots, leave turnips whole, and break broccoli into florets.

Steam veg for 5-6 mins, or until cooked to taste Place in baskets and brush with any remaining fat.

TRADITIONAL CHRISTMAS DAY

Make it a real celebration with the best Christmas meal ever. There's Roast Turkey with a delicious Herb & Chestnut Stuffing, Lime-Glazed Carrots & Parsnips, crispy Roast Potatoes and Crunchy Brussels – but do leave room for the Pud!

CRAB & ORANGE MEDLEY

4 medium oranges
12 oz/350 g white crab meat
few drops of Tabasco sauce
¼ pint/150 ml natural Greek yogurt
salt and freshly ground black pepper
1 lettuce, washed and shredded
dill sprigs to garnish

SERVES 8 • CALORIES PER PORTION: 118

Grate rind from one of the oranges and reserve. Using a sharp knife, peel and segment all the oranges, ensuring that pith is removed. Reserve juice and segments. Mix the crab meat with the Tabasco sauce, Greek yogurt and orange rind. Season to taste. Arrange shredded lettuce in the base of 8 glasses, then lightly fold orange segments and juice into crab mixture and spoon on top of lettuce. Garnish.

ROAST TURKEY

10 lb/4.5 kg oven-ready turkey, with
   giblets, thawed if frozen
2 onions, peeled
small bunch of parsley
Herb & Chestnut Stuffing
   (see recipe)
2 tbsp butter or margarine
1 small carrot
2 bay leaves
4 peppercorns

SERVES 8 • CALORIES PER PORTION: 535

Preheat the oven to Gas 4, 350°F, 180°C.

Remove giblets, then wash and dry the turkey inside and out with kitchen paper. Place one onion and the bunch of parsley inside the body cavity of the turkey. Stuff the neck end with the stuffing and secure with a skewer, then spread the turkey with fat. Weigh the stuffed turkey and calculate the cooking time, allowing 20 mins per 1 lb/450 g, plus a further 20 mins.

Place the turkey on a trivet in a large roasting tin, cover with foil and place in the oven. Cook for calculated cooking time, removing the foil 30 mins before the end of the cooking time.

Wash the giblets and place in a saucepan with the remaining onion (quartered), carrot, bay leaves and peppercorns. Cover with 1½ pints/900 ml cold water. Bring to the boil, cover and simmer gently for 45 mins. Strain and use this stock to make Turkey Gravy (see page 59).

HERB & CHESTNUT STUFFING

1 lb/450 g fresh chestnuts, peeled
8 fl oz/250 ml chicken stock
1½ oz/40 g butter or margarine
1 small onion, peeled and finely
   chopped
salt and freshly ground black pepper
4 oz/100 g fresh white breadcrumbs
3 tbsp freshly chopped coriander
1 tsp ground cinnamon

SERVES 8 • CALORIES PER PORTION: 173

Place peeled fresh chestnuts in a saucepan with the stock and cook for 20 mins, or until the chestnuts are tender. Drain well, reserving the stock, then finely chop the cooked chestnuts. Melt the fat in a saucepan, then sauté the onion for 2 mins. Add the chopped chestnuts and season. Stir in the breadcrumbs, chopped coriander, ground cinnamon and enough reserved stock to make a soft consistency. Use to stuff the neck end of the turkey.

LIME-GLAZED CARROTS & PARSNIPS

1 lb/450 g parsnips, peeled and halved
   lengthways
1 lb/450 g carrots, peeled and halved
   lengthways
3 tbsp clear honey
juice and pared rind of 2 limes
fresh parsley sprigs to garnish

SERVES 8 • CALORIES PER PORTION: 65

Preheat the oven to Gas 4, 350°F, 180°C. Remove the core from the parsnips. Place parsnips and carrots in a pan of lightly

salted boiling water and cook for 15 mins. Drain well, then transfer to a shallow ovenproof dish. Pour the honey and lime juice over, sprinkle with pared lime rind. Cover with foil and cook for 30 mins, or until the vegetables are tender. Remove from oven and garnish with parsley sprigs.

SESAME ROASTIES

1½ oz/40 g lard or oil
3 lb/1.5 kg medium-size potatoes, peeled
4 tbsp sesame seeds

SERVES 8 • CALORIES PER PORTION: 213

Preheat the oven to Gas 4, 350°F, 180°C. Heat the lard or oil in a roasting tin in the oven. Make diagonal cuts in the potatoes, ensuring that you don't cut right through. Place in a pan of lightly salted boiling water, and parboil for 15 mins. Drain. Place the potatoes in the heated fat and cook for 1 hr, basting occasionally. Sprinkle with the sesame seeds and cook in the oven for a further 30 mins. Drain and serve.

CRUNCHY-TOPPED BRUSSELS WITH BACON

2 lb/900 g Brussels sprouts
8 oz/225 g smoked back bacon, rind removed
1 oz/25 g fresh white breadcrumbs
1 oz/25 g butter, melted

SERVES • CALORIES PER PORTION: 119

Trim the bases from the Brussels sprouts and discard the outer leaves. Wash and shake dry. Cut a small cross in the base of each sprout. Place them in a pan of lightly salted boiling water and cook for 10-15 mins, or until tender. Drain thoroughly, place in a serving dish, cover and keep warm.

Roughly chop the bacon, then place in a frying pan and cook for 5 mins, or until crispy. Drain. Add the breadcrumbs and butter to the pan and cook for a further 2-3 mins, stirring constantly. Sprinkle the bacon and breadcrumbs over the sprouts and serve.

SAUSAGEMEAT CASTLES

2 lb/900 g pork sausagemeat
6 oz/190 g jar cranberry sauce
2 tbsp freshly chopped sage
cranberries and sage leaves to garnish

SERVES 8 • CALORIES PER PORTION: 382

Preheat the oven to Gas 4, 350°F, 180°C. Lightly grease eight dariole moulds. Mix the sausagemeat with the cranberry sauce and freshly chopped sage. Season. Divide the mixture between the prepared moulds, cover and chill until required.

Bake in the oven for 15 mins, or until set. Carefully remove the sausagemeat from the moulds, drain off excess liquid, then place on a lightly greased baking sheet. Return to the oven and cook for a further 10 mins, or until browned. Garnish with the cranberries and sage leaves, and serve with the turkey.

TURKEY GRAVY

6 tbsp turkey juices from roasting tin
2½ oz/65 g plain flour
1½ pint/900 ml giblet stock
few drops of gravy browning
2-3 tbsp dry sherry

MAKES 1½ PINT/900 ML • SERVES 8
CALORIES PER 1 FL OZ/25 ML: 15

Heat the turkey juices in a pan. Stir in the flour and cook for 2-3 mins. Remove the pan from the heat. Stir in the giblet stock and season. Mix in the gravy browning and sherry. Return the pan to the heat and cook for a further 2-3 mins and stir until thickened.

VICTORIAN BOXING DAY

The Big Day's gone but the partying is far from over...treat your family to some delicious Victorian delights, and round off Christmas in perfect style!

CRUDITES & DIP

FOR THE CRUDITES:
8 oz/225 g carrots, peeled
8 oz/225 g broccoli florets, washed
8 oz/225 g cauliflower florets, washed
FOR THE DIP:
8 tbsp reduced-calorie mayonnaise
4 tbsp low-fat natural yogurt
4 tbsp pesto sauce
basil sprig to garnish

SERVES 8 • CALORIES PER PORTION: 123

Slice the carrots into thin sticks and arrange on a serving platter with the broccoli and cauliflower.

For the dip, mix together the mayonnaise, natural yogurt and pesto sauce and place in a serving bowl. Serve garnished with the basil sprig and accompanied by the prepared vegetables.

RATATOUILLE

3 tbsp olive oil
2 garlic cloves, peeled and crushed
1 large onion, peeled and sliced
1 large yellow pepper, deseeded and sliced
1 large red pepper, deseeded and sliced
1 large green pepper, deseeded and sliced
1 large aubergine, diced
2 x 14 oz/397 g cans chopped tomatoes
3 tbsp tomato purée
2 tsp mixed herbs
salt and freshly ground black pepper
12 oz/350 g open-cap mushrooms, wiped and halved

SERVES 8 • CALORIES PER PORTION: 78

Heat oil in a large pan and sauté garlic, onion and peppers for 3-4 mins. Add aubergine and cook for a further 2 mins. Then stir in the tomatoes, tomato purée, herbs and seasoning, bring to boil and simmer for 30-40 mins.

Finally, add the mushrooms to the pan and continue to cook for a further 10 mins, until all the vegetables are tender and the sauce is thick. Serve.

BABY BAKED POTATOES

2 lb/900 g baby potatoes, scrubbed
3 tbsp sunflower oil
1-2 tbsp coarse sea salt
freshly ground black pepper

SERVES 8 • CALORIES PER PORTION: 141

Preheat the oven to Gas 6, 400°F, 200°C. Place the baby potatoes in a baking tin, pour the oil over and season according to taste. Bake for 45-55 mins, until potatoes are tender. Serve.

BEEF & WALNUT CASSEROLE

2 lb/900 g stewing steak, trimmed and cubed
3 tbsp plain flour
salt and freshly ground black pepper
2 tbsp sunflower oil
12 oz/350 g baby onions, peeled
½ pint/300 ml stout
1 pint/600 ml rich beef stock
3 bay leaves
10 oz/300 g jar pickled walnuts, drained
6 oz/175 g walnut halves
bay leaves to garnish

SERVES 8 • CALORIES PER PORTION: 489

Toss cubed beef in the flour with seasoning until well coated. Heat oil in a large pan and fry beef and onions for 4-5 mins, until sealed and browned all over. Pour in stout and stock. Bring to the boil, cover and simmer for approx 10 mins.

Add bay leaves and pickled walnuts, cover and cook over a gentle heat for 2-2½ hrs.

Stir in the walnut halves and continue cooking for a further 30 mins-1 hr, or until tender, rich and dark. Serve the casserole garnished with bay leaves.

TIPSY TRIFLE

FOR THE CUSTARD:
1 vanilla pod, or 2 tsp vanilla essence
1 pint/600 ml milk
6 egg yolks, size 3
4 tbsp caster sugar
1 tbsp cornflour
FOR THE TRIFLE BASE:
6 almond macaroons
2 tbsp raspberry jam
40 ratafia biscuits
¼ pint/150 ml dessert wine or sweet sherry
4 pineapple slices
TO FINISH:
1 pint/600 ml double cream
finely grated rind of 1 lemon
silver dragees and frosted rose petals to decorate

SERVES 8 • CALORIES PER PORTION: 557

To make the custard, place the vanilla pod (if using) and the milk in a pan and bring to the boil. Remove from heat and stand for 30 mins. Remove and discard pod.

Whisk together the egg yolks, sugar, cornflour and vanilla essence, if using, and gradually blend in milk. Strain into a double boiler, or a bowl placed over a pan of simmering water, then cook, stirring, until thickened. Allow the mixture to cool completely.

Meanwhile, spread the macaroons with

raspberry jam and place in base of large trifle bowl. Top with ratafias and pour wine or sherry over, then arrange the pineapple slices on top. Pour the cooled custard over and leave until properly set.

Whisk the double cream until just peaking and gently fold in the lemon rind. Spread half of the cream over the custard and place remaining cream in a piping bag fitted with a large star nozzle. Pipe rosettes round the edge of the trifle. (If you don't have a piping bag, you can just spoon the cream round the edge instead.) Finally, decorate the trifle with dragees and rose petals and serve immediately.

If you prefer, you can replace the pineapple slices with 6 oz/175 g raspberries, thawed if frozen. Likewise, the macaroons can be replaced by slices of Madeira or sponge cake.

PORT JELLY

4 oz/100 g caster sugar
4 oz/100 g redcurrant jelly
1½ pint/900 ml ruby port
1 oz/25 g powdered gelatine
mint sprigs to decorate

SERVES 8 • CALORIES PER PORTION: 274

Place the sugar and jelly in a pan and add ¼ pint/150 ml water. Heat gently until the sugar has dissolved and jelly has melted. Stir in the ruby port. Dissolve gelatine in 4 tbsp boiling water and stir into the port mixture.

Pour into a wetted 2 pint/1.2 litre jelly mould and leave overnight in fridge until completely set.

To serve, dip the mould in some hot water for a few seconds and invert on to a

Clockwise from top left: Baby Baked Potatoes; Ratatouille; Beef & Walnut Casserole; Tipsy Trifle; Stilton cheese, dates and grapes; Port Jelly; Crudités & Dip

serving plate. Decorate the jelly with the mint sprigs and serve accompanied by a few grapes, Stilton cheese, dates and assorted nuts.

HANDY TIPS

If preferred you can substitute the ruby port with either red wine or cranberry juice. If using cranberry juice, cut the amount of caster sugar down to 2 oz/50 g and then proceed as above.

TRADITIONAL BOXING DAY

Serve up some quick and easy treats on Boxing Day. They look simply delicious and taste even better! Your family and friends won't be able to wait to tuck in to the feast.

MELON IN PORT

1 honeydew melon
1 small water-melon
3 pieces of stem ginger
1 tsp ground cinnamon
¼ pint/150 ml ruby port
stem ginger to garnish (optional)

SERVES 6 • CALORIES PER PORTION: 80

Halve the honeydew melon and the water-melon and remove the seeds. Using a melon-baller, scoop out the flesh and place in a bowl. Slice the stem ginger and add to the melon with the ground cinnamon and port. Cover and chill in the fridge for 3-4 hrs, stirring occasionally.

Transfer to a large serving dish, garnish with stem ginger, if using, and serve.

PEPPERED MACKEREL

6 smoked mackerel fillets
1 oz/25 g butter or margarine, softened
6 tbsp mixed-coloured peppercorns, crushed
FOR THE SAUCE:
4 tbsp creamed horseradish
¼ pint/150 ml low-fat natural yogurt
4 small dill cucumbers, chopped
1 tbsp capers
grated rind of ½ lemon
dill cucumbers, fresh dill sprigs and lemon wedges to garnish

SERVES 6 • CALORIES PER PORTION: 491

Wash the mackerel fillets and pat dry carefully with kitchen paper. Spread the butter or margarine over the fillets. Place the crushed peppercorns on a sheet of greaseproof paper, then roll the mackerel in the peppercorns, ensuring that fillets are completely covered. Cover and chill in the fridge for 20 mins.

To make the sauce, mix the creamed horseradish with the yogurt. Stir in the dill cucumbers, capers and lemon rind. Cover and chill in the fridge for 10 mins.

Arrange the mackerel on a serving plate, garnish with dill cucumbers, fresh dill sprigs and lemon wedges, and serve with the prepared horseradish sauce.

TURKEY & HAM POT

1½ lb/675 g cooked turkey meat
1 lb/450 g ham
2 tbsp vegetable oil
8 oz/225 g carrots, peeled and sliced
2 large onions, peeled and quartered
¾ pint/450 ml chicken stock
¼ pint/150 ml rosé wine
2 tbsp tomato purée
8 oz/225 g broccoli florets
3 oz/75 g French beans, thawed if frozen
2 tbsp freshly chopped chives
salt and freshly ground black pepper
4 tbsp cornflour
2 tbsp low-fat natural yogurt
freshly chopped chives to garnish

SERVES 6 • CALORIES PER PORTION: 381

Preheat the oven to Gas 4, 350°F, 180°C. Cut the turkey and ham into 1 in/2.5 cm cubes. Heat the oil in a frying pan, then sauté the carrots and onions for 5 mins. Drain well and place in a 5 pint/2.75 litre casserole dish. Add the turkey and ham to the casserole, then pour in the chicken stock and wine. Stir in the tomato purée, cover and cook in the oven for 30 mins. Stir in the broccoli, French beans and the chopped chives. Season to taste. Cook for a further 15 mins, then remove from the oven. Blend the cornflour with 4 tbsp cold water, stir into casserole and continue to cook for 10 mins, or until thickened. Stir in natural yogurt and garnish to serve.

PARSLEYED RICE

12 oz/325 g brown rice
salt and freshly ground black pepper
3 tbsp freshly chopped parsley

SERVES 6 • CALORIES PER PORTION: 198

Place the rice in a pan of lightly salted boiling water. Boil gently for 30 mins, or until cooked. Drain well. Season to taste, then add parsley and mix well. Place in a warmed serving dish to serve.

NUT & MUSHROOM CREAM

1 tbsp vegetable oil

1 oz/25 g butter or margarine

1 onion, peeled and sliced

2 garlic cloves, peeled and crushed

1 green pepper, deseeded and
   thinly sliced

1 red pepper, deseeded and
   thinly sliced

4 oz/100 g baby sweetcorn

8 oz/225 g whole almonds, blanched

8 oz/225 g filberts or hazelnuts
   shelled and blanched

4 oz/100 g unsalted cashew nuts

2 tbsp freshly chopped coriander

4 oz/100 g small oyster mushrooms

FOR THE SAUCE:

1½ oz/40 g butter or margarine

1½ oz/40 g flour

½ pint/300 ml dry white wine

½ pint/300 ml milk

2-3 tsp English mustard

salt and freshly ground black pepper

¼ pint/150 ml double cream

fresh coriander sprigs to garnish

SERVES 6 • CALORIES PER PORTION: 666

Heat the oil and the butter or margarine in a heavy-based frying pan. Sauté the onion and garlic for 2-3 mins. Add the peppers and the baby sweetcorn, and cook for a further 5 mins. Add the nuts, coriander and mushrooms, then continue to cook for 5 mins. Keep warm.

To make the sauce, melt the butter or margarine in a pan, stir in the flour and cook for 1 min. Gradually blend in the dry white wine and milk to form a smooth thick sauce. Add the mustard, season to taste and continue to cook, stirring throughout, for 2-3 mins. Pour the sauce over the nut mixture, then add the cream and stir well. Transfer to a serving dish, garnish and serve.

ICED MINCE TARTS

FOR THE PASTRY:

1 lb/450 g flour

pinch of salt

4 oz/100 g butter or margarine

4 oz/100 g lard or white vegetable fat

2 tsp ground cinnamon

FOR THE FILLING:

1¼ lb/550 g mincemeat

3 tbsp brandy

1½ tsp ground cinnamon

1 egg, size 3, beaten

3 oz/75 g icing sugar, sieved

MAKES 12 • CALORIES PER PORTION: 423

Preheat the oven to Gas 5, 375°F, 190°C. Sieve flour into a mixing bowl with salt. Rub in butter or margarine and lard or vegetable fat, until the mixture resembles breadcrumbs. Stir in cinnamon, then add 6 tbsp water and bring together to form a smooth dough. Wrap and chill for 20 mins.

Roll pastry out on a lightly floured surface to a ¼ in/6 mm thickness. Cut out twelve 4 in/10 cm rounds and use to line Yorkshire pudding tins. Cut the remaining pastry into ¼ in/6 mm wide strips.

To make the filling, mix mincemeat, brandy and cinnamon in a bowl. Use to fill tart cases, brush pastry edges with egg. Twist pastry strips and place across tarts, trimming to fit. Brush with the remaining egg. Bake for 15-20 mins, or until pastry is golden. Leave in tins for 5 mins, then remove and cool on a wire rack.

Mix icing sugar with sufficient hot water to form a thin, smooth icing. Drizzle over the pies and allow to set before serving.

CHRISTMAS STAR

1 lb/450 g puff pastry, thawed if
   frozen

1 egg, size 3, beaten

2 lb/900 g green dessert apples,
   cored and sliced

1 tbsp lemon juice

1 tsp grated nutmeg

1 oz/25 g caster sugar

1 lb/450 g frozen raspberries, thawed
   and drained

apple and raspberries, to decorate

SERVES 6 • CALORIES PER PORTION: 295

Preheat oven to Gas 6, 400°F, 200°C. Roll out half the pastry on a lightly floured surface to a ¼ in/6 mm thickness. Cut out a four-pointed star shape. Place on a dampened baking sheet, brush edge with egg. Roll out remaining pastry and cut out another star, the same size. Using a sharp knife, cut out centre of star, leaving a 1 in/2.5 cm rim. Place rim on top of complete star and press edges firmly together, then knock up sides. (Use left-over pastry to make extra mince pies!) Bake for 20 mins, reduce oven temperature to Gas 4, 180°C, 350°F, and cook for 20-25 mins, or until golden.

Meanwhile, cook apples, lemon juice, nutmeg and sugar with 2 tbsp water until softened. Stir in raspberries. Remove pastry star from oven and leave to stand for 5 mins. Place on a serving platter. Fill pastry case with apple and raspberry mixture. Decorate to serve.

VEGETARIAN CHRISTMAS

Try these mouthwatering festive vegetarian recipes as a healthy alternative to the traditional Christmas meal. They're really tasty as well as being easy to cook and prepare.

PINE NUT ROAST

1½ oz/40 g butter or margarine
2-3 tbsp dried breadcrumbs
1 onion, peeled and finely chopped
2 garlic cloves
2 oz/50 g pine nuts
4 oz/100 g unsalted cashew nuts, finely chopped
2 oz/50 g ground almonds
4 oz/100 g fresh brown or white breadcrumbs
grated rind 1 large lemon
4 tbsp milk
2 eggs, size 3, beaten
salt and freshly ground black pepper
½-1 tsp grated nutmeg
FOR THE STUFFING:
4 oz/100 g butter or margarine, softened
grated rind and juice 1 lemon
1 tsp dried thyme
4 tbsp freshly chopped parsley
1 garlic clove, peeled and crushed
4 oz/100 g fresh brown breadcrumbs
TO GARNISH:
2 tbsp pine nuts, toasted,
lemon slices and parsley sprigs

SERVES 6 • CALORIES PER PORTION: 524

Preheat the oven to Gas 4, 350°F, 180°C, 10 mins before cooking the Roast. Line a 9 x 5 x 3 in/23 x 12.5 x 7.5 cm loaf tin with non-stick baking parchment paper then lightly grease the paper with ½ oz/15 g of the butter or margarine and coat with the dried breadcrumbs.

Melt the remaining fat in a pan, add the onion and garlic and sauté over a gentle heat for 7 mins or until soft and lightly browned. Remove from the heat then mix in the nuts, breadcrumbs, lemon rind, milk and eggs. Season to taste with the salt, pepper and nutmeg. Stir until thoroughly mixed together. Make the stuffing by blending all the ingredients into the softened fat.

Spoon half the nut mixture into the prepared loaf tin and top with the stuffing, levelling out the top. Cover with the remaining nut mixture. Smooth the surface, cover with foil then place on a baking sheet.

Cook in the oven for 50-55 mins, remove the foil and continue to cook for a further 5-10 mins or until browned. Remove from the oven and leave for 5 mins before turning out on to a serving plate.

Discard the lining paper and sprinkle with the toasted pine nuts. Serve garnished with lemon slices and parsley sprigs.

COURGETTE RATATOUILLE

4 tbsp olive oil
2 large onions, peeled and sliced
1-2 garlic cloves, peeled and crushed
1-2 red peppers, deseeded and sliced
1 green or yellow pepper, deseeded and sliced
1 lb/450 g courgettes, trimmed and sliced
salt and freshly ground black pepper
1-2 tbsp white wine or wine vinegar
1 tbsp freshly chopped parsley

SERVES 6 • CALORIES PER PORTION: 110

Heat the oil in a frying pan then add the onions and garlic and fry over a gentle heat for 10 mins or until soft and lightly golden. Add the peppers and continue to fry, stirring occasionally for a further 5-7 mins or until the peppers are soft. Add the courgettes, salt and pepper to taste and the wine or vinegar then stir the mixture lightly together. Cook over a gentle heat for 5-7 mins, stirring frequently until the courgettes are cooked but still crisp. Check seasoning then serve sprinkled with the chopped parsley and serve hot or cold with wholemeal or rye bread.

Left to right: Parsnip Duchesse Potatoes; Pine Nut Roast with Spicy Tomato Sauce; Courgette Ratatouille

SPICY TOMATO SAUCE

8 fl oz/250 ml tomato ketchup
9 fl oz/275 ml red wine
salt and freshly ground black
 pepper
1-2 garlic cloves, peeled and crushed
1 tsp mixed dried herbs
½ tsp caster sugar

MAKES ½ PINT/300 ML
CALORIES PER 1 FL OZ/25 ML: 124

Blend the ketchup and wine together then place in a saucepan with salt and black pepper, garlic, mixed herbs and sugar. Bring to the boil and simmer, uncovered, for about 10 mins or until the sauce is thick enough to coat the back of a spoon. Adjust the seasoning then serve with the Pine Nut Roast.

PARSNIP DUCHESSE POTATOES

1½ lb/675 g parsnips, peeled and cut
 into chunks
1½ lb/675 g potatoes, peeled and cut
 into chunks
salt and freshly ground black pepper
¼ tsp freshly grated nutmeg
1 egg, size 3, beaten

SERVES 6 • CALORIES PER PORTION: 153

Preheat oven to Gas 4, 350°F, 180°C, 15 mins before baking the potatoes. Lightly grease a baking sheet.

Cook the parsnips and potatoes in boiling salted water for 15-20 mins or until soft, drain thoroughly then mash until smooth. Pass through a fine sieve to ensure there are no lumps. Season with the salt, pepper and nutmeg then beat in the egg to form a piping consistency. Spoon the mixture into a piping bag fitted with a large star nozzle and pipe large whirls on to a greased baking sheet. Bake in the oven for 35 mins or until lightly browned. (They may be prepared earlier in the day and left covered. If cooking from cold increase the cooking time by 5 mins.)

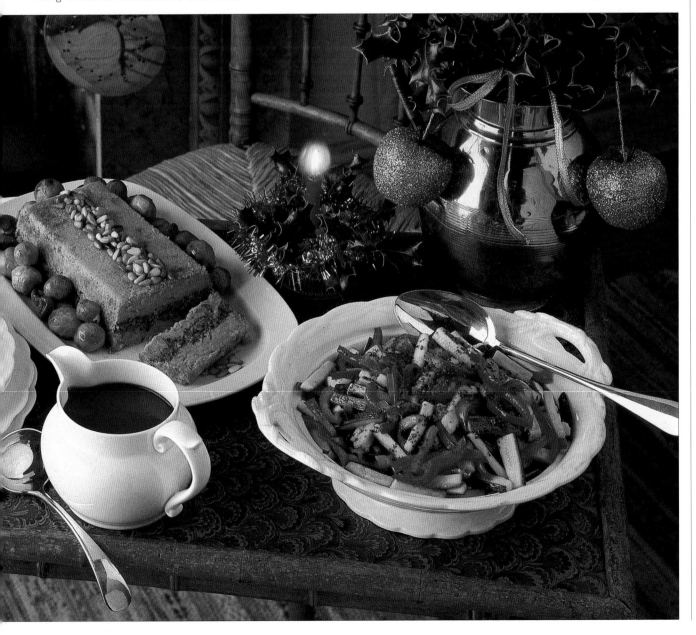

NEW YEAR'S EVE MEAL

Welcome in the New Year in traditional Hogmanay style. Here's a range of unusual dishes to try, each with the flavour of Scotland. The food is hearty and exceptionally good, so raise a glass and let's drink a toast to the New Year!

COCK-A-LEEKIE

2½ lb/1.25 kg oven-ready chicken

1 onion, peeled and sliced

2 bay leaves

few parsley sprigs

1 lb/450 g leeks, washed, trimmed

3 pints/1.7 litres chicken stock

3 oz/75 g long-grain rice

4 oz/100 g no-need-to-soak prunes

salt and freshly ground black pepper

SERVES 8 • CALORIES PER PORTION: 238

Wash the chicken, place in a large pan with the onion, bay leaves and parsley sprigs. Cut leeks into rings, place half in the pan and reserve remainder. Add the stock to pan, bring to the boil, cover, then simmer for 2 hrs, or until chicken is tender.

Remove the chicken, discard skin and bones, cut flesh into small chunks. Skim off any fat from top of cooking liquid, then return chicken to pan with rice and prunes.

Bring to the boil, then simmer for 20 mins. Add the remaining leeks, season to taste, and continue to simmer for 10 mins, or until leeks are tender.

CRANACHAN

2 oz/50 g oatmeal

1 pint/600 ml double cream

2-3 tbsp Drambuie

clear honey to taste

12 oz/350 g raspberries, hulled if fresh, thawed if frozen

SERVES 8 • CALORIES PER PORTION: 354

Place the oatmeal in a heavy-based frying pan over a moderate heat. Cook, stirring, until lightly toasted. Leave until cold. Whip cream until softly peaking, then stir in Drambuie. Pile into individual glass dishes and sprinkle a little oatmeal on top.

To serve, drizzle honey over cream with extra oatmeal, mix lightly and top with raspberries.

POACHED SALMON

4 lb/1.75 kg whole salmon, cleaned

1 onion, peeled and sliced

1 lemon, sliced

2 sticks celery, trimmed and sliced

few parsley stalks

2 bay leaves

¼ pint/150 ml medium-dry white wine

lemon slices, salad leaves and fresh chervil to garnish

SERVES 8 • CALORIES PER PORTION: 405

Wash the salmon thoroughly and pat dry with kitchen paper. Leave the scales on to keep salmon intact and make it easier to skin.

Place the onion, lemon, celery, parsley and bay leaves in a fish kettle or a large saucepan. Add the wine with 1½ pint/900 ml water. Bring to boil, then simmer for 10 mins. Place salmon on fish kettle trivet or a piece of foil folded over twice, and gently lower into simmering liquid. Bring to a gentle boil, reduce heat and cover pan. Cook for 8 mins.

Remove from heat, then allow fish to cool completely in the liquid. When cold, remove fish from pan. Carefully remove the skin from both sides of fish, then discard gills and eyes. Using a pair of scissors, snip the backbone at the head and tail, then carefully ease out the bone. Place the fish on serving platter and garnish with lemon, salad and chervil. (The salmon need not be boned – this will help to keep it intact – just make sure guests know bones are there.)

CLOOTIE DUMPLING

8 oz/225 g self-raising flour

4 oz/100 g shredded vegetable suet

1 tsp baking powder

4 oz/100 g medium oatmeal

4 oz/100 g light soft brown sugar

1 tsp ground cinnamon

½ tsp grated nutmeg

½ tsp ground ginger

4 oz/100 g sultanas

4 oz/100 g raisins

2 oz/50 g cut mixed peel

2 tbsp golden syrup or black treacle

2 eggs, size 3, beaten

4 fl oz/120 ml milk

SERVES 8 • CALORIES PER PORTION: 590

Dust a pudding cloth with flour or line the base of a 2 pint/1.2 litre pudding basin with greaseproof paper and lightly grease. Sieve the flour into a mixing bowl, then add all dry ingredients, fruit and mixed peel. Warm the syrup or treacle and beat into the eggs. Pour into dry ingredients, and mix with sufficient milk until mixture forms a soft consistency.

If using a pudding cloth, place mixture in the centre, then tie loosely together to allow room for expansion. If using a basin, place mixture in basin, smooth top then cover with greaseproof paper and foil. Secure firmly.

To boil the dumpling: if using a pudding cloth, place in a large saucepan half-filled with boiling water and boil gently for 3-3½ hrs, replenishing water as necessary. If using a basin, place in a steamer over a pan of boiling water, steam for 3-3½ hrs.

To serve: if boiled in the cloth, dip the pudding in a bowl of cold water for

Clockwise from bottom: Poached Salmon, garnished with lemon, salad and chervil; Clootie Dumpling; Cranachan; Black Bun; Cock-a-Leekie; Shortbread

10 seconds, then turn out on to a heat-proof plate and dry in a hot oven for 5 mins. If cooked in basin, turn on to warmed serving plate. Serve with custard.

Traditionally, the pudding is cooked in a pudding cloth. When turned out it has a skin formed by boiling in the floured cloth.

SHORTBREAD

6 oz/175 g plain flour
4 oz/100 g butter, softened
2 oz/50 g caster sugar
2 oz/50 g almonds, chopped finely
8 whole blanched almonds
caster sugar for dredging

MAKES 8 SLICES
CALORIES PER PORTION: 250

Preheat the oven to Gas 4, 350°F, 180°C. Sieve flour into a mixing bowl, add the butter, sugar and chopped almonds. Working with your hand, bring ingredients together to form a smooth dough, leaving

sides of bowl clean. Place on a lightly floured surface and knead until smooth.

Roll out to a 7 in/18 cm circle approx ¼ in/6 mm thick. Slide on to a baking sheet and smooth round edge to form a neat circle. Pinch together with thumb and forefinger to give a decorative finish, then prick lightly with a fork.

Arrange the whole almonds on top, then bake for 25-30 mins or until lightly golden. Remove from oven and mark into eight portions, dredge lightly with the caster sugar. Allow to cool completely before cutting right through.

BLACK BUN

12 oz/350 g prepared shortcrust pastry
8 oz/225 g plain flour
1 tsp cream of tartar
1 tsp bicarbonate of soda
1 tsp ground cinnamon
1 tsp ground ginger
1/2 tsp freshly grated nutmeg
12 oz/350 g seedless raisins
12 oz/350 g currants
4 oz/100 g cut mixed peel
4 oz/100 g chopped mixed nuts
4 oz/100 g soft brown sugar

1 egg, size 3
¼ pint/150 ml whisky
2-3 tbsp milk
beaten egg or milk to glaze

CUTS INTO 12 SLICES
CALORIES PER SLICE: 635

Preheat the oven to Gas 4, 350°F, 180°C. Lightly grease an 8 in/20 cm, deep cake tin. Reserve a third of the pastry, then roll out remainder and use to line cake tin, easing the pastry into sides of tin and to top. Trim.

Sieve flour, cream of tartar, bicarbonate of soda and spices into a large mixing bowl. Add fruit, mixed peel, nuts and sugar, mix well.

Beat egg with the whisky, then add to mixture. Mix with enough milk to give a moist consistency. Spoon into the pastry-lined tin, packing down firmly with the back of a spoon.

Roll out remaining pastry, cut a lid to fit tin, dampen edges, then place on top of mixture. Seal edges firmly. Using a skewer, pierce the bun 4 times, right through to the base, then prick top with a fork. Brush with beaten egg or milk and bake for 2-2½ hrs. During cooking, brush the top with egg or milk. Remove from the oven and cool in tin.

NEW YEAR'S DAY MEAL

The perfect meal for New Year's Day – with delicious Lamb in Filo Pastry served with Pommes Parisienne and Courgette Ratatouille and followed by a choice between Choc'n'Orange Soufflé and Ruby Red Pudding.

MUSHROOMS A LA GRECQUE

12 oz/350 g button mushrooms
1 medium onion
1 garlic clove
8 oz/225 g firm tomatoes
1 tbsp olive oil
7 fl oz/200 ml dry white wine
2 bay leaves
juice of ½ lemon
salt and freshly ground black pepper
1 tsp caster sugar
1 tsp coriander seeds
fresh chervil sprigs to garnish

SERVES 6 • CALORIES PER PORTION: 106

Wipe the mushrooms and if very large, cut in half. Peel and finely chop the onion, peel and crush the garlic clove. Wash and dry the tomatoes, cut into quarters, deseed and finely chop. Heat the oil in a frying pan then sauté the onion and garlic for 5 mins or until soft and transparent. Add the mushrooms, tomatoes, wine, bay leaves, lemon juice, salt and pepper, sugar and coriander seeds and cook gently for approx 10 mins or until the mushrooms are just cooked. Remove from the heat, cover and chill for at least 3 hrs or overnight if preferred. Discard the bay leaves, arrange in a serving dish and garnish with chervil sprigs.

LAMB IN FILO PASTRY

1 small leg of lamb, approx 2½ lb/
   1.25 kg in weight, boned
salt and freshly ground black pepper
FOR THE STUFFING:
1 small onion, peeled and finely
   chopped
1 celery stick, trimmed and finely
   chopped
1 tbsp olive oil
3 oz/75 g fresh white breadcrumbs
grated rind and juice of 1 lime
3 oz/75 g shelled hazelnuts, skinned
   and finely chopped
2 tbsp freshly chopped mint
1 egg, size 5, beaten
FOR THE PASTRY:
8 sheets filo pastry
2 oz/50 g butter, melted
lime wedges and mint sprigs to
   garnish

SERVES 6 • CALORIES PER PORTION: 519

Preheat the oven to Gas 4, 350°F, 180°C, 10 mins before roasting the lamb.
Wipe the lamb and discard any excess fat. Season with the salt and pepper. Cover and leave to one side.

To prepare the stuffing, gently sauté the onion and celery in the oil for 5 mins or until soft then remove from the heat. Add the breadcrumbs, lime rind and juice, hazelnuts, mint and seasoning. Mix well then bind together with the beaten egg to form a stiff consistency. Use to stuff the lamb in the cavities left from the removal

of the bones. Shape any remaining stuffing into small balls and place in oven to cook with the lamb for the last 20 mins of cooking time. Tie to a neat shape to encase the stuffing. Place in a roasting tin then roast in the oven for 1½ hrs. Remove from the oven and allow to become cold then discard the string.

Preheat the oven to Gas 6, 400°F, 200°C, 15 mins before cooking the lamb in the filo pastry. If necessary trim the lamb to a good shape before covering with the pastry. (Remember when using filo pastry to keep it wrapped in clearwrap so that it does not dry out.) Brush one sheet of filo pastry with a little melted butter and place another sheet on top. Brush this with butter then place a third sheet of pastry on top. Repeat with three more sheets of filo pastry. Use these to completely encase the lamb, brushing with butter to seal. Place on a baking sheet and brush with more butter. Cook in the oven for 30 mins or until pale golden brown. Meanwhile cut out small leaves from the remaining two sheets of filo pastry, cover with clearwrap

drain. Heat the oil and butter in a roasting pan, add the potatoes then roast, basting frequently for 35-40 mins or until cooked and golden brown. Drain, toss in the chopped parsley and serve.

CHOC'N'ORANGE SOUFFLE

4 eggs, size 3, separated
3 tbsp caster sugar
grated rind and juice of 1 orange
½ oz/15 g gelatine
½ pint/300 ml whipping cream
6 oz/175 g plain chocolate, grated
40 ratafia biscuits
2 tbsp Cointreau
orange rind to decorate

SERVES 6 • CALORIES PER PORTION: 419

Place the egg yolks, sugar, rind and juice of the orange in a large bowl over a pan of gently simmering water. Whisk until thick, creamy and doubled in volume. Remove from the heat and continue to whisk until cold. Add the gelatine to 3 tbsp very hot water and stir until completely dissolved, allow to cool then pour into the whisked egg mixture in a thin steady stream, stirring as you go. Whip the cream until softly peaking then stir into the soufflé mixture. Whisk the egg white until stiff and standing in peaks then stir in 2 tbsp and mix well. Add remaining egg white and mix lightly together until thoroughly incorporated.

Place a jam jar in the centre of a glass serving dish and spoon a layer of the soufflé around the jar. Cover with a layer of grated chocolate then a further layer of soufflé. Repeat the layers ending with a layer of soufflé then place in the fridge for at least 3-4 hrs, or overnight.

Just before serving, place the ratafia biscuits in a small bowl and pour over the Cointreau. Carefully fill the jam jar with boiling water, leave for 30 seconds then

gently ease the jar out of the centre of the soufflé. Fill the cavity with the soaked ratafia biscuits and decorate the top with the orange rind.

RUBY RED PUDDING WITH BABY MERINGUES

FOR THE MERINGUES:
1 egg white size 3
2 oz/50 g caster sugar
FOR THE PUDDING:
12 oz/350 g blackcurrants, thawed if frozen or 2 x 7 oz/200 g cans of blackcurrants, drained
3 oz/75 g granulated sugar or to taste
3 tbsp port
12 oz/350 g mixed fresh fruit such as grapes, strawberries,
melon and blueberries
mint sprig to decorate

SERVES 6 • CALORIES PER PORTION: 136

Preheat the oven to its lowest setting just before drying out the meringues.

Line a baking sheet with non-stick vegetable parchment. Whisk the egg white until really stiff then add 1 tbsp of the sugar and whisk again until stiff. Add the remaining sugar and fold in using a metal spoon or spatula. Place in a piping bag fitted with a large star nozzle then pipe small rosettes on to the baking sheet. Place in the oven and leave to dry out for 2-3 hrs. (The exact length of time will depend on how hot your oven is.)

To make the Ruby Red Pudding, place the blackcurrants and the sugar in a heavy-based pan with ½ pint/300 ml water. Place over a gentle heat and simmer for 30 mins, stirring occasionally, until the blackcurrants are cooked and the sugar completely dissolved. Remove from the heat, cool slightly then pass through a food processor or liquidizer until smooth. If liked pass the purée through a fine sieve to remove all the pips then stir in the port. Prepare the fresh fruit, cutting it into bite sized pieces then stir into the blackcurrant purée. Cover then leave to cool in the fridge. Place in a serving bowl and serve with the meringues and fresh cream.

or a damp cloth and reserve.

Remove the lamb from the oven and arrange the leaves of filo pastry in a decorative pattern across the top of the pastry, brushing with butter to attach them to the pastry. Brush with a little more butter then return to the oven for a further 5-10 mins or until golden brown. Serve garnished with lime wedges and mint sprigs.

POMMES PARISIENNE

2 lb/900 g potatoes
salt
3-4 tbsp olive oil
1 tbsp butter
freshly chopped parsley

SERVES 6 • CALORIES PER PORTION: 183

Preheat the oven to Gas 6, 400°F, 200°C, 15 mins before baking potatoes. Peel potatoes then using a melon ball cutter scoop out small balls the size of large marbles, alternatively, cut potatoes into large dice. Blanch in boiling salted water then

TEMPTING TEA-TIME RECIPES

Bake up some really special treats with these tasty tea-time recipes. There are loaf sandwiches, fruity Marzipan Fancies, Fruit Horns and a selection of mouthwatering biscuits for a tea they'll love!

LOAF SANDWICHES

¾ oz/20 g butter or margarine
4½ slices fresh wholemeal bread, crusts removed
4½ slices fresh white bread, crusts removed
4 oz/100 g garlic cream cheese
1 tbsp freshly snipped chives
salt and freshly ground black pepper
3 in/7.5 cm piece of cucumber, sliced
2 eggs, size 3, hard-boiled and shelled
3 tbsp mayonnaise
1 carton mustard and cress
watercress and tomatoes to garnish

SERVES 6 • CALORIES PER PORTION: 282

Butter bread and cut whole slices in half lengthways to fit bases of six ¼ pint/150 ml loaf tins. Line bases of three tins with wholemeal bread and three with white. Mix cream cheese and chives, season, then spread half over wholemeal bread in tins. Top with half of the cucumber and another layer of wholemeal bread. Repeat layers once more, topping with a slice of bread, buttered side down. Cover and chill for 1 hr.

Roughly chop the hard-boiled eggs in a bowl. Add mayonnaise, then season to taste and mix well. Repeat the method for the sandwiches above, but using white bread and egg mayonnaise in place of the cream cheese, and mustard and cress in place of the cucumber. Turn out of tins, slice, garnish and serve.

If preferred, use two 1 lb/450 g loaf tins to make 2 large Loaf Sandwiches instead of 6.

CHOCOLATE PIN WHEEL BISCUITS

2½ oz/65 g butter or margarine
3 oz/75 g caster sugar
1 egg, size 5, beaten
2 tsp sherry
pinch of baking powder
5 oz/150 g plain flour
1 tbsp cocoa powder, sieved
grated rind of ½ lemon
1 egg white, size 5, beaten

**MAKES 18 • SERVES 6
CALORIES PER BISCUIT: 81**

Preheat the oven to Gas 5, 375°F, 190°C, 10 mins before baking. Cream fat and sugar in a bowl until light and fluffy, then beat in egg and sherry. Sieve baking powder with flour, then work into the creamed mixture. Divide the mixture in half. Work the cocoa powder into half of the mixture, and lemon rind into other half. Wrap separately and chill for 1 hr.

Roll out both doughs separately on a lightly floured surface to make two 11 in x 5 in/28 cm x 13 cm rectangles. Brush white dough with beaten egg white and place chocolate dough on top. Lightly brush top of the dough with egg white, then carefully roll up from the short end. Wrap and chill for 1 hr.

Using a sharp knife, cut the roll into ¼ in/6 mm thick slices. Place well apart on a baking sheet, to allow for expansion, and bake for 8-10 mins, or until cooked. Leave on a wire rack to cool.

MARZIPAN FANCIES

icing sugar for dusting
12 oz/350 g marzipan
3½ oz/90 g trifle sponges
3 tbsp sherry
4 oz/100 g curd or cream cheese
2 oz/50 g caster sugar
2 oz/50 g canned peach slices in natural juice, drained or 1 orange, peeled and segmented
marzipan flowers to decorate

MAKES 6 • CALORIES PER PORTION: 333

Lightly dust six ¼ pint/150 ml ramekin dishes with icing sugar. Line the base of each with baking parchment. Knead the marzipan, roll out three-quarters on a surface dusted with icing sugar, to a ¼ in/ 6 mm thickness. Cut out six 5 in/13 cm

Clockwise from bottom left: fruity Marzipan Fancies; melt-in-the-mouth Orange Bites, dusted with icing sugar; luxurious Fruit Horns, decorated with angelica and icing sugar; Chocolate Pin Wheel Biscuits; and centre, Loaf Sandwiches, garnished with watercress and tomatoes

to the egg mixture. Fold in gently with a metal spoon. Gently stir in the melted fat and vanilla essence. leave the batter to stand for 15 mins in a cool place.

Fill each mould three-quarters full, then bake in the oven for 10-12 mins, or until risen and golden. Remove from the moulds and leave to cool on a wire rack. Dust with icing sugar to serve.

FRUIT HORNS

8 oz/225 g prepared puff pastry, thawed if frozen
I egg, size 5, beaten
I satsuma, peeled and segmented
3 fl oz/85 ml double cream
angelica and sieved icing sugar to decorate

MAKES 12 • SERVES 6
CALORIES PER HORN: 116

Preheat the oven to Gas 6, 400°F, 200°C. Lightly grease twelve cream horn tins. Roll the pastry out on to a lightly floured surface to a 6 in × 10 in/15 cm × 26 cm rectangle. Cut pastry into twelve ½ in × 10 in/1.25 cm × 26 cm strips. Dampen one edge of each strip and, starting at the tip of the mould, wind a strip around each mould, overlapping the pastry slightly. Continue until all the pastry has been used.

Brush the pastry with beaten egg. Place seam-side down on a dampened baking sheet and bake for 12-15 mins, or until risen and golden. Leave to stand for 5 mins, then remove pastry from tins. Leave to cool on a wire rack.

Cut each satsuma segment in half. Whip the cream until it peaks and fold in the satsumas. Spoon the cream into the pastry cases, then decorate with angelica and dust with icing sugar.

circles and line base and sides of ramekin dishes. Reserve remaining marzipan.

Cut trifle sponges into thin strips. Place three-quarters of the sponge round sides and over base of moulds. Drizzle over 2 tbsp sherry. Cream the curd or cream cheese and caster sugar together. Roughly chop the peach slices, or chop the orange, if using. Add to the cheese mixture and divide between moulds. Top with reserved sponge and drizzle the remaining sherry over the top.

Roll out reserved marzipan and cut out six 3 in/7.5 cm circles. Place on top of moulds, sealing edges. Cover with foil and weigh down with weights. Chill in the fridge overnight.

Using a palette knife dipped in hot water, carefully turn cakes out. Dust with icing sugar and decorate with marzipan flowers.

ORANGE BITES

3½ oz/90 g caster sugar
3 eggs, size 5, beaten
grated rind of I orange
3½ oz/90 g plain flour, sieved
½ tsp baking powder
3 oz/75 g butter or margarine, melted
½ tsp vanilla essence
icing sugar for dusting

MAKES 24 • SERVES 6
CALORIES PER CAKE: 66

Preheat the oven to Gas 6, 400°F, 200°C, 15 mins before cooking. Lightly grease and flour twenty-four 1 fl oz/25 ml cake moulds. Place the sugar and eggs in a bowl and whisk together until thick and creamy. Add the orange rind. Mix the flour and baking powder together and sprinkle on

CHILDREN'S TEA PARTY

Go crazy and take a trip to Wonderland with Alice and her friends! It's so easy to entertain the kids with these super recipe ideas for the perfect tea party. They're also great for a birthday or just a friendly get-together.

WHITE RABBIT SANDWICHES

24 slices thick-sliced soft-grain bread
2 tbsp low-fat spread
4 tbsp wholenut peanut butter
6 tbsp reduced-calorie coleslaw
4 tbsp seedless raisins, chopped
2 cartons mustard and cress, washed and trimmed
3 oz/75 g grated carrot
sliced carrot, green pepper and pitted black olives to garnish

MAKES 12 • CALORIES PER SANDWICH: 114

Using a rabbit cutter or template, cut out one rabbit from each slice of bread (bread scraps can be made into breadcrumbs and frozen for use in burgers, toppings, stuffings, etc.), Spread low-fat spread on one side of each rabbit shape. Spread twelve with peanut butter, then top with coleslaw and raisins. Cover each with remaining rabbit shapes and press together lightly.

Mix together mustard and cress and grated carrot, then divide between two serving plates. Garnish each sandwich with carrot strips for jackets, pepper strips for boots and pieces of olive for buttons and eyes. Serve on the prepared salad. Cover lightly with clearwrap until ready to serve.

FOB WATCH PIZZAS

2 x 5.1 oz/145 g packets of wholemeal pizza base mix
4 fl oz/120 ml ready-made pizza topping
3 oz/75 g reduced-fat Cheddar cheese, grated
thinly sliced pitted black olives, green pepper strips and
cherry tomatoes to garnish

MAKES 12 • CALORIES PER PIZZA: 74

Preheat the oven to Gas 6, 400°F, 200°C, 15 mins before baking the pizzas. Combine the pizza base mixes together, then add sufficient water, following the instructions on the packet, to form a firm dough. Turn dough on to a lightly floured surface, then knead thoroughly until smooth. Roll dough out to a thickness of ¼ in/6 mm, then, using a 3 in/7.5 cm round cutter, stamp out twelve circles, re-rolling as necessary.

Place dough circles on greased baking sheets, spread each with pizza topping and sprinkle with cheese. Leave in a warm place to rise for 15 mins, then bake for 15-20 mins, or until golden. Leave on tray until required.

To garnish the pizzas, arrange twelve olive slices around the edge of each pizza to form hour markers and two pepper strips in the centre to represent the hands of a watch face. Transfer to serving plates and garnish with the cherry tomatoes. Serve warm or cold.

TOADSTOOL MERINGUES

3 egg whites, size 3
6 oz/175 g caster sugar
4 tbsp white icing or buttercream
2 tsp powdered drinking chocolate for dusting

MAKES 12 • CALORIES PER MERINGUE: 80

Preheat the oven to Gas 2, 300°F, 150°C, 5 mins before baking. Whisk egg whites until very stiff and whisk in half the sugar until glossy. Using a large metal spoon, fold in the remaining sugar. Place meringue mixture in a large piping bag fitted with a plain ½ in/1.25 cm nozzle. Pipe twelve 2 in/5 cm diameter 'mushroom tops' on to a baking sheet lined with baking parchment and, on another lined sheet, pipe twelve 1 in/2.5 cm 'stalks'. Bake for 40-50 mins, or until lightly browned. Leave to cool on baking sheets, then peel away from the baking parchment.

Secure the stalks to tops with icing or buttercream and place on serving plate. Dust with drinking chocolate to serve.

PLAYING CARD HOUSE

10 oz/300 g plain flour
6 oz/175 g butter or margarine
2 oz/50 g ground almonds
3 oz/75 g caster sugar
1 egg, size 3, beaten
10 oz/300 g fondant icing
1 tbsp clear honey
few drops natural red food colouring
2 tbsp white icing
few drops of black food colouring

MAKES 12 BISCUITS
CALORIES PER BISCUIT: 350

Preheat the oven to Gas 4, 350°F, 180°C, 10 mins before baking biscuits. Sieve flour into a bowl, then rub in fat until mixture resembles breadcrumbs. Stir in the ground almonds, sugar, beaten egg and enough water to form a firm dough.

Knead on a lightly floured surface until smooth, then roll out to a 10 in x 10½ in/26 cm x 27 cm rectangle. Divide into twelve 2½ in x 3½ in/6.5 cm x 9 cm rectangles and place on lightly greased baking sheets. Chill for 30 mins, then bake for 12-15 mins, or until firm and lightly browned. Allow to cool on trays for 10 mins, then transfer to a wire rack to cool completely.

Thinly roll out 7 oz/200 g fondant icing and cut into twelve 3 in x 2 in/7.5 cm x 5 cm rectangles. Brush each biscuit with honey and secure a fondant rectangle on top of each.

Clockwise from bottom left: Fob Watch Pizzas, garnished with black olives and green pepper; Toadstool Meringues, dusted with drinking chocolate; Playing Card House; Fruits of the Forest Punch; more Toadstool Meringues; and White Rabbit Sandwiches, garnished with carrot, green pepper and black olives

Colour remaining fondant icing with red food colouring, then roll and cut out enough heart shapes for twelve heart playing cards – ace to 9 then Jack, Queen and King. For the ace, Jack, Queen and King, cut out a large heart each, plus four small hearts. Position hearts as in a deck of cards and secure each one with honey.

Colour half the white icing with black food colouring, then place in a small piping bag fitted with a writing nozzle and use to define the Jack, Queen and King cards by piping a 'J', 'Q', 'K' on to three of the large hearts. Leave icing to dry.

To assemble the house, spread some of the remaining icing along the bottom edge of four biscuits, lean two against each other to form a triangle and secure on serving plate. Repeat with other two biscuits and place alongside on plate.

Spread more icing on the top of each triangle and lay a biscuit between the two stacks. Place two more biscuits on top to form another triangle, securing in place with the rest of the icing as you go. Arrange the other biscuits around plate and allow icing to dry before serving.

FRUITS OF THE FOREST PUNCH

1¼ pint/750 ml cranberry and raspberry juice, chilled
½ pint/300 ml reduced-calorie blackcurrant juice, chilled
¾ pint/450 ml sparkling apple juice, chilled
raspberries and red and green skinned apple slices to float

SERVES 6 • CALORIES PER PORTION: 161

Pour the fruit juices into a serving bowl and mix well. Stir in the fruit. Ladle both punch and fruit into cups to serve.

BUFFET LUNCH

Entertaining is as much a part of Christmas as Santa Claus. Here is a sumptuous array of easy-to-follow recipes devised to create a memorable buffet table.

TUNA CHEESECAKE

4 oz/100 g cream cracker biscuits
3 oz/75 g low-fat spread
FOR THE FILLING:
2 x 7 oz/200 g cans line-caught
   tuna in brine
1 lb/450 g fromage frais
grated rind and juice of 2 limes
3 celery sticks, trimmed and
   finely chopped
1 tbsp anchovy essence
2 tbsp freshly snipped chives
¼ oz/11 g sachet gelatine
lemon or lime slices and chervil
   sprigs to garnish

SERVES 6 • CALORIES PER PORTION: 276

Lightly grease the base and sides of an 8 in/20.5 cm loose-bottomed cake tin. Roughly crush cream cracker biscuits. Melt the low-fat spread, then add to the crushed biscuits and mix well. Use to cover the base of the greased tin, pressing the mixture down firmly with the back of a metal spoon. Chill until set.

Meanwhile, make the filling. Drain the tuna and flake finely with a fork, then place in a mixing bowl with the fromage frais, lime rind and juice, chopped celery, anchovy essence and snipped chives. Mix well.

Dissolve the gelatine in 3 tbsp hot water, stir until completely dissolved. Cool, then add to the tuna mixture, pouring it in gently in a thin steady stream, using a metal spoon or spatula in a figure of eight movement. Ensure that the filling is thoroughly mixed. Spoon mixture into the tin and chill for at least 3-4 hrs, or until set.

When ready to serve, carefully remove cheesecake from the tin. Decorate with the lemon or lime slices and chervil sprigs.

If preferred, the tuna can be substituted with canned salmon.

VEGETABLE RICE MOULD

½ pint/300 ml vegetable stock
2 tsp agar agar
2 oz/50 g French beans
2 small carrots
8 oz/225 g long-grain rice
1 small red pepper
2 tbsp pumpkin seeds
3 tbsp freshly chopped coriander
yellow and red cherry tomatoes
tarragon sprig to garnish

SERVES 6 • CALORIES PER PORTION: 176

Heat vegetable stock to boiling point and stir in the agar agar until dissolved. Leave to cool.

Top and tail the beans, cut into 1 in/ 2.5 cm pieces, then blanch in boiling salted water for 3 mins. Drain and refresh by plunging into cold water. Leave until cold.

Peel the carrots and cut into 1 in/2.5 cm matchsticks. Blanch in boiling salted water for 2 mins, then plunge into cold water. Leave until cold, then drain. Dry vegetables with kitchen paper, then mix together and arrange in the base of a damp 2 pint/1.2 litre ring mould. Add enough stock to cover vegetables, then leave to set on a bed of ice.

Cook the rice in boiling salted water for 12-15 mins, or until cooked. Drain, rinse thoroughly with hot water.

Deseed the pepper and chop finely. Mix the chopped pepper, pumpkin seeds and coriander into the rice with any remaining stock. Pack into mould on top of the set vegetables and smooth the top with a palette knife. Chill for 2 hrs.

When ready to serve, quickly dip the mould into a bowl of hot water, invert on to a serving plate and carefully remove mould. Fill centre with cherry tomatoes, and garnish with the tarragon sprig.

FRUIT TERRINE

4 tbsp ginger wine
2 tbsp agar agar
1 bottle medium-sweet white wine
1 large Charentais or Galia melon
6 oz/175 g seedless green grapes
fresh strawberries to decorate

SERVES 6 • CALORIES PER PORTION: 159

Heat the ginger wine to boiling point, then sprinkle in agar agar and blend to a paste. Stir in the white wine and mix well. Return to the heat and stir until the mixture is smooth. Pour a little of the wine mixture into a 2 lb/900 g loaf tin to a depth of ¼ in/6 mm. Leave to set.

Cut the melon in half, scoop out the seeds, then peel and cut into thin slices. Wash and dry the grapes. Arrange the melon slices side by side, with peeled edge facing down, on the set jelly in the tin. Chop any remaining melon into chunks and use, with 4 oz/100 g grapes, to fill the loaf tin. Add remaining wine mixture, then chill overnight until set.

To serve, dip the terrine into a bowl of hot water for 2-5 secs, then carefully ease mixture away from the sides of the tin. Decorate with the remaining grapes and strawberries.

APRICOT SOUFFLE

8 oz/225 g no-need-to-soak apricots
juice and rind of 1 lemon
4 eggs, size 1, separated
4 oz/100 g caster sugar
¼ oz/11 g sachet gelatine
½ pint/300 ml whipping cream
1 oz/25 g flaked almonds
mint sprigs and extra no-need-to-
   soak apricots to decorate

SERVES 6 • CALORIES PER PORTION: 366

Tie a double band of greaseproof paper around a 6 in/15 cm soufflé dish, ensuring that the paper stands at least 2 in/5 cm above the top of the dish.

Place the apricots in a small pan with the lemon juice, rind and ¼ pint/150 ml water. Bring to the boil, then poach gently for 10 mins, or until soft and pulpy. Remove from the heat and put through a processor to form a smooth purée. Leave to cool.

Meanwhile, place egg yolks and caster sugar in a bowl over a pan of gently simmering water and whisk until pale, thick and creamy (the whisk should leave a trail on the surface when lightly pulled across the top). Remove from the heat and con-

tinue to whisk until the mixture is cold. Stir apricot purée into mixture.

Dissolve the gelatine in 4 tbsp water, then add to the mixture in a thin, steady stream.

Whip the cream until softly peaking, then gently fold into the mixture. Whisk the egg whites until stiff, then add 3 tbsp to the mixture and fold in carefully with a metal spoon. Fold in the remaining egg white in the same way. (Adding the egg white in stages, folding it in gently each time, means that as little air as possible is lost from the mixture.)

Turn into the prepared soufflé dish and smooth the top. Chill for at least 3 hrs, or until set.

When ready to serve, carefully peel away the band of greaseproof paper, using a round-bladed knife if necessary, then press almonds on to sides of soufflé. Decorate the top with the mint sprigs and extra apricots.

Clockwise from top left: Tuna Cheesecake; Apricot Soufflé; Fruit Terrine; Vegetable Rice Mould

MICROWAVE MEAL

Microwave cooking is really easy and, once you've had a little practice, you'll soon be dishing up some delicious dishes for your family and friends – in minutes. So let's get microwaving with these mouthwatering recipes.

MIXED BEAN SOUP

3 oz/75 g dried mung beans

3 oz/75 g dried aduki beans

2 oz/50 g dried black-eyed beans

1 tbsp olive oil

1 garlic clove, peeled and crushed

1 medium onion, peeled and chopped

1 stick celery, chopped

1 carrot, peeled and diced

¾ pint/450 ml vegetable stock

¾ pint/450 ml tomato juice

salt and freshly ground black pepper

1 tbsp freshly chopped coriander

4 tbsp low-fat natural yogurt

coriander sprigs to garnish

SERVES 4 • CALORIES PER PORTION: 276

Place mung, aduki and black-eyed beans in a large microwaveable bowl. Cover with 1 pint/600 ml cold water. Cover and cook on High for 15 mins. Leave to cool. Drain and rinse. Pour ½ pint/300 ml boiling water over beans, cover and cook on High for 12 mins. Leave to stand for 1 hr. Drain if necessary.

Meanwhile, place oil in another bowl and heat on High for 30 secs. Add garlic, onion, celery and carrot. Cover and cook on High for 3-4 mins. Add beans, stock, and tomato juice, then season and stir in coriander. Cover and cook on Medium for 30 mins.

Pour into four bowls and top each with 1 tbsp natural yogurt. Garnish with sprigs of coriander.

WARM TROUT SALAD

1 lb/450 g baby new potatoes, scrubbed

3 tbsp sunflower oil

1½ tbsp raspberry vinegar

salt and freshly ground black pepper

1 tsp clear honey

1 lb/450 g trout fillets, skinned

2 tbsp white wine

½ small cucumber, sliced

2 tbsp capers

1 radicchio lettuce, washed, leaves separated

few leaves oak leaf lettuce, washed

2 small dill sprigs

1 tbsp pine nuts

SERVES 4 • CALORIES PER PORTION: 374

Put potatoes into a medium-sized microwaveable bowl with 2 tbsp water. Cover and cook on High for 8-10 mins, until tender, stirring occasionally.

Meanwhile, make the dressing. Place oil, vinegar, seasoning and honey in a small screw-top jar and shake to mix. Drain potatoes and pour dressing over. Put aside. Slice the trout fillets into thin ½ in/1.25 cm strips and place in a shallow dish with the wine. Cover and cook on High for 3 mins. Stand for 1 min. Drain trout, if liked.

Arrange the sliced cucumber, capers, radicchio and oak leaf lettuce on a serving dish. Spoon potato mixture over, then add the trout. Sprinkle with dill and pine nuts. Serve immediately with crusty bread.

MOUSSAKA-STYLE LOAF

1 lb/450 g minced lean lamb

salt and freshly ground black pepper

1 lb/450 g large courgettes, washed

1 small aubergine

2 tbsp olive oil

1 medium onion, peeled and finely chopped

½ tsp caster sugar

15 oz/425 g can chopped tomatoes

2 tsp tomato purée

2 tsp freshly chopped rosemary

1 egg, size 3, beaten

3 oz/75 g Cheddar cheese, grated

rosemary sprigs and tomato wedges to garnish

SERVES 4 • CALORIES PER PORTION: 422

Place minced lamb in a microwaveable bowl. Cover the dish and cook on High for

Clockwise from bottom left: Mixed Bean Soup; Warm Trout Salad; Caramel Apple Pudding; Moussaka-Style Loaf and centre, Choc'n'Orange Fudge Bars

lamb, along with the rosemary and beaten egg.

Line a greased 2 lb/900 g microwaveable loaf tin with some of the courgette slices, overlapping them slightly to ensure there are no gaps. Spoon half the lamb mixture into base, arrange aubergine on top. Sprinkle cheese over and top with remaining lamb. Cover with remaining courgettes, tuck in ends and trim as necessary.

Cover dish lightly and cook on Medium for 15 mins. Stand for 5 mins. Pour the remaining tomato sauce into a microwaveable jug. Heat on High for 30 seconds until hot. Pour off any juices from loaf and turn out on to a serving dish.

Garnish loaf with rosemary and tomato wedges, and serve sliced with the tomato sauce.

CARAMEL APPLE PUDDING

4 oz/100 g plain flour
4 oz/100 g dark brown sugar
pinch of cinnamon
3 oz/75 g butter or margarine
6 medium dessert apples
1 tbsp lemon juice
mint sprigs and lemon zest to decorate

SERVES 4 • CALORIES PER PORTION: 489

Sieve the plain flour into a bowl, stir in 2 oz/50 g dark brown sugar and cinnamon. Rub in 1 oz/25 g fat until the mixture resembles breadcrumbs. Stir in 1-2 tbsp cold water to form a firm dough. Wrap and chill for 1 hr.

Place the remaining fat in a microwaveable 8 in/20 cm round pie dish and heat on High for 45 secs. Sprinkle the remaining dark brown sugar over. Peel, core and thickly slice the apples. Sprinkle with lemon juice. Arrange the apple slices in the base of the pie dish.

Roll out the dough to fit over the apples and press down lightly. Cook on High for 7-10 mins, until the surface feels dry. Stand for 5 mins.

Loosen with a knife, invert a serving plate on to the pie dish, turn upside down

on the plate. Remove pie dish and decorate top of pudding with mint sprigs. If liked, serve with crème fraîche decorated with lemon zest.

CHOC'N'ORANGE FUDGE BARS

4½ oz/120 g butter or margarine
4½ oz/120 g plain chocolate
14 oz/400 g caster sugar
4 eggs, size 3, beaten
4 oz/100 g plain flour
finely grated rind of 1 orange
pinch of salt
3 oz/75 g chopped walnuts
1 oz/25 g white chocolate
orange zest to decorate

MAKES 15 • CALORIES PER BAR: 300

Grease and line an 11 in x 9 in/28 cm x 23 cm microwaveable baking dish. Place fat and plain chocolate in a microwaveable bowl and heat on High for 1½-2 mins until melted, stirring once. Remove from oven, stir until smooth. Beat in sugar and eggs. Sieve and stir in flour, orange rind and salt until well mixed. Pour into the prepared baking dish.

Elevate dish on rack or upturned ramekins and cook on High for 3 mins. If your oven is too small for the baking dish to rotate, it may be necessary to invert the turntable to stop it turning. Sprinkle chopped walnuts over and continue to cook for 5-6 mins, until just set, turning the dish halfway through cooking.

It is most important that you do not overbake; the mixture should still look slightly undercooked – it will finish cooking out of the oven. Allow to cool, then cover and refrigerate.

Place white chocolate in a small bowl and melt on High for 1 min. Drizzle the melted chocolate over the cold fudge mixture. Allow to set before slicing into fifteen bars. Decorate with orange zest before serving.

Note: always use dishes, plates and bowls that are suitable for cooking in microwaves. Avoid any which have a metal trim.

10 mins, stirring occasionally until cooked. Drain off fat. Season meat and cool.

Using a vegetable peeler, thinly slice the courgettes lengthways then place in a shallow microwaveable dish. Thinly slice the aubergine, add to the dish, then cover and cook on High for 2 mins. Season and leave to cool.

Heat oil in a microwaveable dish on High for 50 secs and stir in onion. Cover and cook on High for 2-3 mins, stirring occasionally, until softened. Stir in sugar, tomatoes and seasoning. Cover and cook for 3 mins more.

Sieve into a bowl and stir in the tomato purée. Mix 4 tbsp tomato sauce into the

COCKTAIL PARTY SNACKS

Fancy a nice nibble? Of course you do! And so will everyone else when they pop in over Christmas. Just look how quick'n'tasty these are!

STUFFED PRUNES

4 oz/100 g cream cheese
I tbsp grated orange rind
salt and freshly ground black pepper
16 pitted no-need-to-soak prunes
16 walnut halves

MAKES 16 • CALORIES PER PORTION: 56

Mix the cream cheese with the orange rind, salt and pepper. Fill each prune with this mixture and top with a walnut half. Serve with cocktails, cheese straws and stuffed olives.

SAUSAGE & BACON KEBABS

7 oz/175 g streaky bacon, derinded
I½ lb/750 g cocktail sausages, pricked
I tbsp olive oil
8 oz/250 g cherry tomatoes

MAKES 12 • CALORIES PER PORTION: 200

Preheat grill. Roll bacon and thread on to kebab sticks with the sausages. Brush lightly with the oil then place under grill and cook, turning occasionally, for 8-10 mins. Skewer a tomato on the end of each.

CHEESE & ONION KEBABS

4 oz/100 g Double Gloucester with chives
6 oz/150 g silverskin pickled onions
8 oz/227 g can pineapple pieces, drained

MAKES 16 • CALORIES PER PORTION: 98

Cut cheese into ½ in/1.25 cm cubes and thread with onions and pineapple on to kebab sticks.

(Try using Cheddar, Stilton or Gouda as a change.)

MELON & PARMA HAM KEBABS

I large ripe honeydew melon, deseeded and peeled
6 oz/175 g Parma ham
8 oz/230 g jar maraschino cherries, drained

MAKES 16 • CALORIES PER PORTION: 60

Cut melon into ½ in/1.25 cm cubes. Wrap half the cubes in Parma ham and thread alternately on to kebab sticks with the plain melon cubes and the maraschino cherries.

VOL-AU-VENTS

20 x 2 in/5 cm vol-au-vents, thawed if frozen
¼ pint/150 ml garlic mayonnaise
¼ cucumber, diced
¼ pint/150 ml crème fraîche
rind of ½ lemon
4 oz/100 g peeled prawns
Tabasco to taste
I tbsp freshly chopped dill
dill sprigs

MAKES 20 • CALORIES PER PORTION: 56

Preheat oven to Gas 7, 425°F, 220°C. Place cases on lightly dampened baking tray and cook for 15-20 mins. Allow to cool. Mix garlic mayonnaise with cucumber and fill half the vol-au-vents. Mix crème fraîche with lemon, prawns, Tabasco and dill; use to fill remaining vol-au-vents. Garnish with chopped cucumber and dill sprigs.

Try using 4 oz/100 g cooked, skinned and finely chopped chicken with the crème fraîche, I tbsp tomato purée and the grated rind of I lime. Alternatively, try tuna mixed with mayonnaise and I finely chopped celery stick.

FESTIVE SAUSAGE ROLLS

I lb/450 g pork sausagemeat
3 tsp creamed horseradish
2 tbsp freshly chopped mixed herbs
salt and freshly ground black pepper
I lb/450 g puff pastry
I egg, size 3, beaten

MAKES 16 • CALORIES PER PORTION: 203

Preheat oven to Gas 6, 400°F, 200°C, 15 mins before baking the sausage rolls. Mix sausagemeat with horseradish, herbs, salt and pepper. Roll pastry to a rectangle 6 in x 16 in/15 cm x 40 cm. Shape sausagemeat roll to the same length and I in/2.5 cm in width. Place in middle of pastry and roll pastry around. Seal with water. Cut into I½ in/4 cm lengths. Slash the tops and place on greased baking tray. Brush with beaten egg. Bake in oven for 20-25 mins.

SATAY NIBBLES

I lb/450 g lamb's liver, trimmed
I lb/450 g boneless chicken breast, skinned
I lb/450 g pork tenderloin, trimmed
12 oz/340 g jar crunchy peanut butter
2 garlic cloves, peeled and crushed
I oz/25 g desiccated coconut
salt and freshly ground black pepper

SERVES 12 • CALORIES PER PORTION: 346

Slice liver, chicken and pork into thin strips; thread on to wooden kebab sticks. Put peanut butter in saucepan with garlic and coconut, seasoning and ¾ pint/450 ml boiling water. Simmer for 10 mins. Marinate meat in sauce for 30 mins. Preheat grill then cook for 10 mins, turning and brushing occasionally with sauce. Serve the nibbles with a yogurt and herb dip.

Clockwise from bottom left: Festive Sausage Rolls; Stuffed Prunes with cheese straws and stuffed olives; Blue Lady; Christmas Cheer; Snowball; Vol-au-Vents; Melon & Parma Ham Kebabs; Cheese & Onion Kebabs; Sausage & Bacon Kebabs, centre, Satay Nibbles served with yogurt & herb dip

SNOWBALL

1 fl oz/25 ml advocaat
1 tbsp lime cordial
lemonade
lemon slices
cocktail cherries

MAKES 1 • CALORIES PER PORTION: 116

Pour advocaat and lime into glass and top up with lemonade. Decorate with lemon and cherries.

BLUE LADY

1 fl oz/25 ml gin
1 fl oz/25 ml blue curaçao
1 tbsp lemon juice

MAKES 1 • CALORIES PER PORTION: 100

Vigorously shake the ingredients together with cracked ice and strain into chilled glass. Add a stuffed olive.

CHRISTMAS CHEER

1 fl oz/30 ml vodka
cranberry and apple juice
cocktail cherry

MAKES 1 • CALORIES PER PORTION: 74

Place the vodka into a chilled glass and top with the cranberry and apple juice. Add a cocktail cherry.

HANDY TIPS

Keep a selection of nibbles handy that you can cook in 20 mins. Why not mix some of your home makes with some of the brand new quick-and-easy products you can find in your local supermarket or food store?
Why not give your guests a glass or two of mulled wine to warm them up when they arrive. Stud 1 orange with approx 2-3 oz/50-75 g light soft brown sugar and 2 lightly bruised cinnamon sticks. Pour in 1 bottle claret and place the bowl either in a microwave or over a pan of gently simmering water and heat through, stirring occasionally. Add 1 pint/600 ml of boiling water and for an extra kick, add 4-6 tbsp of brandy. Stir before serving in heatproof glasses.

CHINESE FEAST

Egg-Fried Rice, Barbecued Ribs, Chicken Chow Mein...we all love them. So here we show you how to prepare your favourite Chinese takeaway dishes that you can cook up quickly and easily in your own home.

CHICKEN CHOW MEIN

4 oz/100 g Chinese egg noodles
2 boneless chicken breasts, each approx 4 oz/100 g in weight
3 tbsp light soy sauce
1 tbsp dry sherry
2 tsp groundnut oil
1 large garlic clove, peeled and bruised
4 oz/100 g button mushrooms, wiped
1 small orange pepper, deseeded and diced
1 small green pepper, deseeded and sliced
4 oz/100 g ham, trimmed and cut into thin strips
4 oz/100 g bean sprouts, rinsed
2 tsp sesame oil

SERVES 4 • CALORIES PER PORTION: 343

Cook the egg noodles in boiling salted water for 5 mins, or until cooked. Drain, then plunge into cold water and leave until completely cold. Drain and reserve.

Discard skin and any fat from chicken. Cut into small chunks and place in a shallow dish. Mix soy sauce with the sherry, then pour over the chicken. Cover and leave to marinate in the fridge for at least 1 hr, turning occasionally. Drain.

Heat the groundnut oil in a wok or large saucepan and fry the garlic for 2 mins. Discard garlic. Add the chicken to the wok or pan and stir-fry for 4 mins until the chicken is completely cooked. Add the mushrooms and peppers, and continue to stir-fry for a further 3 mins. Add the drained noodles, the ham and bean sprouts, then stir-fry for a further 3 mins. Sprinkle with sesame oil, fry for a further 1 min, then serve with prawn crackers.

SESAME PRAWN TOASTS

8 oz/225 g peeled prawns, thawed if frozen
4 small spring onions, trimmed
½ tsp salt
1 egg, size 5
1 tbsp light soy sauce
1 tsp sesame oil
6 slices thinly sliced white bread
1 oz/25 g sesame seeds
oil for deep frying
spring onion tassels to garnish

SERVES 4 • CALORIES PER PORTION: 255

Dry the prawns on kitchen paper. Cut off the green part from the spring onions and discard. Place prawns, spring onions and salt in a food processor and blend until thoroughly chopped. Alternatively, you can do this by using a wooden board and a Chinese cleaver or large kitchen knife.

Add the egg, soy sauce and sesame oil, then blend for 30 secs, or until thoroughly mixed. Trim off crusts from the bread, then discard. Cut bread into 3 in × 1 in/ 7.5 cm × 2.5 cm oblongs. Spread with the prepared prawn mixture and sprinkle generously with sesame seeds.

Heat oil in a wok or deep fat fryer and fry the toasts in batches for 3-5 mins, turning at least once, until golden brown. Drain on kitchen paper and garnish. The Prawn Toasts are best eaten immediately after cooking.

BEEF WITH MANGETOUT

8 oz/225 g fillet steak, trimmed
1 tsp cornflour
1½ tbsp dark soy sauce
1½ tbsp dry sherry
2 tbsp groundnut or vegetable oil
2 in/5 cm piece root ginger, peeled and chopped
6 spring onions, sliced diagonally
1 large carrot, peeled and sliced diagonally
1 red pepper, deseeded and sliced
2½ fl oz/65 ml stock
8 oz/227 g can water chestnuts, drained
4 oz/100 g mangetout, trimmed

SERVES 4 • CALORIES PER PORTION: 208

*Clockwise from top left: Egg-Fried Rice;
Barbecued Ribs; Sesame Prawn Toasts;
Beef with Mangetout; and Chicken
Chow Mein*

then pour over the ribs. Cover and leave
to marinate in the fridge for at least 4 hrs,
turning occasionally.

Drain ribs, reserving marinade. Place in
a roasting tin and cook for about 45 mins,
basting with marinade and turning at least
twice. Serve garnished with parsley and
radishes.

EGG-FRIED RICE

4 oz/100 g long-grain rice
6 spring onions
4 oz/100 g smoked bacon
1 tbsp groundnut or vegetable oil
**3 oz/75 g peeled prawns, thawed and
   dried, if frozen**
3 oz/75 g frozen peas, thawed
1 egg, size 3, beaten
mangetout to garnish

SERVES 4 • CALORIES PER PORTION: 206

Cook the rice in boiling salted water for
12-15 mins, or until cooked. Drain, rinse
thoroughly in cold water, then drain again.
Leave until completely cold.

Trim and discard green part of spring
onions. Chop remainder. Discard any rind
from bacon and cut meat into small pieces.
Heat the oil in a wok or large pan, then fry
onions and bacon for 2 mins. Add the rice,
then stir-fry for 4 mins, or until heated
through. Stir in prawns and peas and
continue to stir-fry for 2 mins. Pour in
beaten egg and stir-fry rapidly for a further
2 mins, or until egg is cooked. Garnish with
a few mangetout.

HANDY TIPS

**The secret of succesful Chinese
cooking is PREPARATION.
Trim and cut all the vegetables in
advance and leave covered until
ready to cook. Prepare the meat and
fish, cutting it finely and discarding
any gristle and fat. Cook rice earlier
in the day, drain, rinse and cover.
Reheat when required.**

Cut the steak into thin strips, then place in
a shallow dish. Mix the cornflour with
½ tbsp soy sauce and ½ tbsp dry sherry,
then pour over the beef, coating the meat
thoroughly. Cover, then leave to marinate
for at least 30 mins.

Heat the oil in a wok or large pan, then
fry the ginger for 3 mins. Discard ginger.
Add the beef to the oil and stir-fry for
3 mins, or until completely sealed. Using a
slotted spoon, remove and reserve the
meat. Stir-fry the onions, carrot and pepper for 2 mins, then return the beef to the
wok or pan and mix well. Add the remaining soy sauce, dry sherry and the stock to
the beef and vegetables and continue to
stir-fry for a further 3-4 mins, or until the
meat is cooked and tender. Add the
drained water chestnuts and mangetout,
stir-fry for 2 mins, then serve straightaway.

BARBECUED RIBS

8 belly of pork ribs
2 in/5 cm piece root ginger
1 tsp sesame oil
4 tbsp Hoisin sauce
1 tbsp oyster sauce
1 tbsp clear honey
2 tbsp dry sherry
**flat leaf parsley and radish roses to
   garnish**

SERVES 4 • CALORIES PER PORTION: 283

Preheat the oven to Gas 5, 375°F, 190°C,
10 mins before cooking. Trim the pork
ribs, discarding any fat or cartilage, and
place in a shallow dish. Peel root ginger
and grate finely, then place in a pan with
sesame oil, Hoisin and oyster sauces,
honey and sherry. Heat through. Stir well,

TRADITIONAL FRENCH FARE

Traditional French cooking is so easy when you know how. Try this meaty Pâté de Campagne, tender chicken cooked with garlic, and, for a special treat, delicious Gâteau Paris-Brest.

PATE DE CAMPAGNE

8 oz/225 g unsmoked streaky bacon, derinded

8 oz/225 g streaky pork rashers, derinded and chopped

8 oz/225 g chicken livers, washed

8 oz/225 g pig's liver, tubes removed, washed and chopped

1 lb/450 g boneless chicken, skinned

2 shallots, peeled and chopped

2 eggs, size 3, beaten

2 garlic cloves, peeled and crushed

2 oz/50 g fresh white breadcrumbs

1 tsp pink peppercorns, drained

1 tsp green peppercorns, drained

5 juniper berries, crushed

3 tbsp freshly chopped parsley

2 oz/50 g pistachio nuts

pinch of nutmeg

1½ tsp salt

freshly ground black pepper

3½ fl oz/90 ml dry white wine

2 tbsp brandy (optional)

2 bay leaves

bay leaves, pink and green peppercorns, cherry tomatoes and parsley to garnish

---

CUTS INTO 12 SLICES
CALORIES PER SLICE: 250

Preheat the oven to Gas 4, 350°F, 180°C, 10 mins before baking. Using the back of a knife, stretch each rasher of streaky bacon. Line a 3 lb/1.5 kg terrine or loaf tin with streaky bacon, arranging it widthways across the tin and overlapping each rasher. Chill.

Meanwhile, place pork rashers, chicken livers, pig's liver, boneless chicken, shallots, eggs and garlic in a processor and blend for 20-30 secs, or until mixed. Pour into a mixing bowl and beat in breadcrumbs, peppercorns, juniper berries, parsley, pistachio nuts and nutmeg. Season. Mix in

wine and brandy, if using. Cover and chill for 1-2 hrs, to allow flavours to develop.

Spoon the mixture into bacon-lined tin, then lay bay leaves on top. Stand in a large roasting pan and fill pan with water to a depth of 1 in/2.5 cm. Bake for 1½ -1¾ hrs, or until a skewer inserted into the middle of the pâté comes out clean and hot, and any juices that run out are clear. Stand the tin on a wire rack and cool for 1 hr. Remove the bay leaves. Cover with greaseproof paper and lay weights on the top. Leave to chill overnight.

Remove pâté from tin, garnish with fresh bay leaves, peppercorns and tomatoes. Serve pâté sliced with French bread and garnished with parsley.

CHICKEN WITH 40 GARLIC CLOVES

3 lb/1.5 kg oven-ready free-range chicken

sea salt and freshly ground black pepper

2 sprigs each of chervil, tarragon, parsley, rosemary and thyme

2 bay leaves

4 tbsp olive oil

40 garlic cloves, unpeeled

1 tbsp fennel seeds

fresh herbs and watercress to garnish

SERVES 4 • CALORIES PER PORTION: 266

Preheat the oven to Gas 4, 350°F, 180°C. Wash and dry chicken, then place in a large oval casserole with a tight-fitting lid. Rub seasoning over chicken.

Take a sprig of each herb and tie them together in a bunch with string. Repeat with the remaining herbs, so that you have two bouquet garnis. Place one bouquet garni in chicken cavity and other in casserole. Mix together oil, garlic cloves and fennel seeds, and spoon over chicken.

Cover casserole with foil, then replace lid. Bake for 1¼ hrs, or until the chicken is tender and cooked.

Remove chicken from casserole and place on a platter. Discard bouquet garnis. Surround chicken with garlic cloves and garnish. Serve chicken sliced with a few cooked garlic cloves.

GATEAU PARIS-BREST

FOR THE CHOUX PASTRY RING:

5 oz/150 g strong plain flour

4 oz/100 g butter

1 tsp salt

4 eggs, size 3, beaten

1 egg, size 5, beaten

2 tbsp flaked almonds

FOR THE FILLING:

5 egg yolks, size 5

4 oz/100 g caster sugar

2 oz/50 g plain flour

13 fl oz/375 ml milk

4 tsp instant coffee

½ oz/15 g butter

1 tbsp icing sugar for dusting

8 oz/225 g strawberries, washed and halved

SERVES 8 • CALORIES PER PORTION: 394

Preheat the oven to Gas 6, 400°F, 200°C. To make the pastry, sieve strong plain flour on to a plate. Place fat in a pan with ½ pint/300 ml water, then heat until boiling. Quickly add the flour and salt, remove from the heat and beat mixture until thick and glossy.

Transfer dough to a large mixing bowl. Using a wooden spoon or an electric mixer, gradually beat in the four size 3 eggs, to form a shiny mixture (it should just fall from a spoon but hold its shape).

Place the dough in a piping bag fitted with a ¾ in/2 cm plain nozzle. Pipe a

10 in/25.5 cm ring on to a dampened baking sheet. Pipe another ring just inside it and then a third ring on top of the other two. Brush with beaten size 5 egg and sprinkle with flaked almonds. Bake in oven for 35-40 mins, or until risen and golden brown. Transfer to a wire rack, and slice horizontally to allow the steam to escape. Leave to cool.

Meanwhile, prepare the filling. In a heatproof bowl, beat the egg yolks and caster sugar until thick and pale. Stir in flour. Heat milk and coffee until just boiling, then whisk into egg mixture. Place bowl over a pan of boiling water and cook, stirring, for 10-15 mins, or until mixture is thick. Heat for 2 mins more, whisking throughout. Remove from heat, dot surface with butter to prevent a skin forming, and leave to cool.

To assemble, remove top from choux ring. Spoon the filling into a piping bag fitted with a ½ in/1.25 cm star nozzle and pipe over choux base (filling should show at the sides). Replace the choux top, dust with icing sugar and fill centre with strawberries. Serve.

Clockwise from left: Chicken with 40 Garlic Cloves; Basque Cake; Gâteau Paris-Brest; Pâté de Campagne

BASQUE CAKE

FOR THE PASTRY:
10 oz/300 g plain flour
7 oz/200 g butter, softened
1 egg, size 3
2 egg yolks, size 3
7 oz/200 g icing sugar, sieved
finely grated rind of 1 lemon
FOR THE FILLING:
9 fl oz/275 ml milk
3 egg yolks
5 oz/150 g caster sugar
3 tbsp plain flour
3 tbsp rum
1 egg, size 5, beaten
1 tbsp icing sugar for dusting
lemon slices to decorate

CUTS INTO 12 SLICES
CALORIES PER SLICE: 395

Preheat the oven to Gas 4, 350°F, 180°C, 10 mins before baking. Lightly grease and flour an 8 in/20.5 cm round, 2 in/5 cm deep, loose-bottomed cake tin.

To make pastry, sieve the flour into a bowl and make a well in the centre. Place butter, egg and yolks, icing sugar and lemon rind into the well and, using fingertips, mix together, gradually drawing in the flour, until the dough is soft and pliable. Form the dough into a ball, wrap and chill for 1 hr.

Meanwhile, prepare the filling. Heat the milk until just about to boil. Whisk together egg yolks and caster sugar until thick and pale. Beat in the plain flour, then gradually whisk in the milk. Pour the mixture into a large saucepan and cook over a low heat, stirring throughout, until thick (take care that you don't burn the mixture). Stir in the rum and allow to cool, whisking occasionally.

Roll out two-thirds of the chilled pastry on a lightly floured surface to fit into the prepared cake tin. Press into tin, so that the pastry slightly overhangs the sides. Next, pour the cooled filling into the tin. Roll out the remaining pastry to form a lid, then place on top. Dampen the pastry edges and pinch together. Chill for 30 mins.

Brush the top of the cake with the beaten egg and bake for 1 hr or until risen, golden and firm to the touch. If the pastry browns too quickly, cover with foil to stop it burning. Allow the cake to cool in the tin, then carefully transfer to a serving plate. Dust with icing sugar and serve decorated with the lemon slices.

SPANISH FARE

Spain is well known for the sun...and the food is wonderful, too! Soak up the fabulous flavours and serve them up a taste they'll love, with delicious dishes to tempt the whole family!

TAPAS SELECTION

Dish up a classic...there's Potato Omelette, Calamares Fritos, Chorizo and Tomatoes with Anchovies.

CALAMARES FRITOS

8 oz/225 g prepared squid, cut
   into rings
3 tbsp plain flour
1 egg, size 3, beaten
oil for deep frying
salt
lemon slices to garnish

SERVES 4 • CALORIES PER PORTION: 212

Rinse and dry the squid. Dust with flour, then dip in egg. Heat oil to 350°F 180°C, and fry squid for 3-4 mins, or until golden. Drain on kitchen paper. Sprinkle with salt. Serve hot with lemon slices.

POTATO OMELETTE

1 large potato, about 10 oz/300 g in
   weight, peeled and thinly sliced
2 tbsp olive oil
¼ Spanish onion, peeled and chopped
1 garlic clove, peeled and chopped
2 eggs, size 3, beaten
salt and freshly ground black pepper
chopped parsley to garnish

SERVES 4 • CALORIES PER PORTION: 157

Place potato in a small omelette pan with the oil. Add the onion and garlic and cook, stirring, over a low heat until the potato is tender but not brown – about 15 mins. Add the eggs and seasoning. Keeping the heat low, cook until the egg has set, then slide the omelette on to a plate, then invert it back into the pan. Continue to cook until firm. Serve warm or cold, cut into small pieces, sprinkled with parsley.

TOMATOES WITH ANCHOVIES

1 large beef tomato
2 oz/50 g can anchovies, drained
ground black pepper

SERVES 4 • CALORIES PER PORTION: 92

Wipe and slice the tomato, arrange on plate. Roll anchovy fillets and place 1 on each tomato slice. Season with black pepper.

CHORIZO

8 oz/225 g chorizo sausage, sliced
   into 12 pieces
2 tbsp olive oil
3 small slices white bread, quartered
12 stuffed green olives

SERVES 4 • CALORIES PER PORTION: 318

Place chorizo sausage in a pan. Heat gently until the juices start to run out. Drain on kitchen paper and reserve. Add oil to pan and fry bread for 2-3 mins. Using cocktail sticks, spear a piece of sausage on to each piece of bread and top with an olive. Serve.

PIRI PIRI PORK

FOR THE PORK:
1½ lb/675 g lean pork fillet
2 garlic cloves, peeled
2 tbsp olive oil
FOR THE SAUCE:
3 red chillis
1 tsp coarse sea salt
¼ pint/150 ml olive oil
2 fl oz/50 ml cider vinegar

SERVES 4 • CALORIES PER PORTION: 361

Slice pork fillet into 2 in/5 cm long thin strips and place in a shallow dish. Crush 1 garlic clove and mix with the olive oil, pour over the pork, cover and chill overnight.

To make the sauce, remove and discard the stems from two chillis, then chop roughly (including the seeds). Place in a small screw-top jar with the salt, oil and vinegar. Seal, shake well and store at room temperature until required (it will keep for up to one month).

Preheat the grill to medium. Drain pork, discarding oil, place in grill pan and grill for 6-7 mins, turning occasionally, or until the meat is tender and brown. Thinly slice the remaining garlic and mix with the pork. Shake the sauce before serving and pour into a small bowl so that the pork can be dipped before eating. Garnish sauce with the remaining chilli. Serve with a green salad and cornbread to take away the fire!

The Piri Piri sauce can be served with any sort of meat, fish or shellfish.

PAELLA

4 small chicken quarters, skinned
salt and freshly ground black pepper
4 tbsp olive oil
4 oz/100 g chorizo sausage
2 Spanish onions, peeled and finely
   chopped
2 garlic cloves, peeled and finely
   chopped
2 red peppers, deseeded and chopped
10 oz/300 g risotto rice, washed
2 tbsp freshly chopped parsley
1 bay leaf
¼ tsp saffron strands
1 pint/600 ml chicken stock
8 oz/225 g cooked mussels, shells
   removed
8 oz/225 g cooked shelled prawns
3 oz/75 g peas, thawed if frozen
4 king prawns, cooked
chopped parsley and slice of lemon to
   garnish

SERVES 4 • CALORIES PER PORTION: 702

Clockwise from bottom left: Piri Piri Pork, served with sauce and green salad; Paella, garnished with parsley and lemon; Sangria; Churros, served with cinnamon sugar. And centre, tasty Tapas Selection (clockwise from bottom left) – Chorizo; Calamares Fritos; Tomatoes with Anchovies; Potato Omelette

Wash and dry the chicken, then season with salt and freshly ground black pepper. Heat 3 tbsp of the olive oil in a paella pan or large frying pan and sauté the chicken until golden brown on both sides. Remove from the pan and keep warm.

Add chorizo sausage, onions, garlic and peppers to the pan and sauté for 10 mins, or until the vegetables are soft. Stir in the rice, parsley, bay leaf and saffron. Add the stock, stir, then simmer, uncovered, for 10 mins.

Return chicken to the pan with the mussels, shelled prawns, peas and king prawns. Cover tightly and cook over a low heat until the rice is tender and all the liquid has been absorbed. Leave to stand, covered, for 10 mins. Serve paella straight from the pan, garnished with parsley and lemon.

CHURROS

1 tsp salt
8 oz/225 g plain flour
1 egg, size 3, beaten
oil for deep frying
½ tsp ground cinnamon
2 oz/50 g caster sugar

SERVES 4 • CALORIES PER PORTION: 424

Place 16 fl oz/475 ml water in a saucepan with the salt. Bring to the boil, then add the flour (all at once) and beat until the mixture forms a ball. Cool slightly, then beat in the egg.

Heat the oil for deep frying to 350°F, 180°C. Place churros mixture in a piping bag fitted with a ½ in/1.25 cm star nozzle and pipe 3 in/7.5 cm lengths into the oil – about four at a time. Fry for 2-3 mins, or until golden, then drain on kitchen paper and transfer to a serving bowl.

Mix cinnamon and sugar, then place in separate bowl for dipping. Serve churros immediately. (If liked, serve the Churros with either a home-made chocolate or butterscotch sauce.)

SANGRIA

1 bottle Spanish red wine
½ pint/300 ml lemonade
2 peaches, stoned and sliced
1 lemon, sliced
1 orange, sliced
1 cinnamon stick, bruised

SERVES 8 • CALORIES PER PORTION: 164

Mix wine and lemonade in a large jug. Add some ice cubes, the sliced fruit and the cinnamon. Serve immediately.

ITALIAN MAGIC

Discover the true taste of Italy with these delicious recipes! There's a wonderful Ricotta Cheesecake, fresh Tomato and Mozzarella Salad, Marsala Figs and the best Calzone pizza ever.

TOMATO & MOZZARELLA SALAD

4 beefsteak tomatoes
8 oz/225 g mozzarella cheese, sliced
few fresh basil leaves
5 tbsp olive oil
salt and freshly ground black pepper
2 oz/50 g pitted black olives
I garlic clove, peeled and thinly
    sliced (optional)

SERVES 4 • CALORIES PER PORTION: 324

Wash, dry and slice the tomatoes. Arrange the mozzarella on a serving plate with the tomato slices . Roughly tear the basil leaves and sprinkle over the salad. Pour the olive oil over the salad, then season with salt and freshly ground black pepper. Top with the black olives and sliced garlic if using.

SPAGHETTI ALLA CARBONARA

I tbsp olive oil
4 fresh sage leaves
I garlic clove, peeled
4 oz/100 g prosciutto ham, or lean
    ham, thinly sliced, or smoked
streaky bacon, derinded and
    thinly sliced
12 oz/350 g spaghetti
3 eggs, size 3, beaten
5 tbsp freshly grated Parmesan
    cheese
salt and freshly ground black pepper
2 oz/50 g butter
about 4 tbsp dry white wine or
    vegetable stock
fresh sage to garnish

SERVES 4 • CALORIES PER PORTION: 414

Heat the olive oil in a large frying pan with the sage and garlic for 1-2 mins. Add the prosciutto ham, lean ham or smoked streaky bacon, then sauté for about 10 mins, or until golden brown. Discard the sage and garlic.

Cook the spaghetti in a large pan of boiling water for about 10 mins, or until al dente – just cooked, but slightly firm.

In a bowl, mix together the eggs and Parmesan cheese, then season to taste. Drain the spaghetti, then return to the saucepan and toss in the butter. Add the spaghetti to the meat in the frying pan and cook for 1 min, stirring throughout.

Remove the pan from the heat, then add the egg mixture and enough wine or stock to give a smooth texture to the sauce. Cover and leave to stand for 2-3 mins (the heat from the spaghetti will cook the eggs – they will take on a scrambled appearance). Mix well and serve immediately, garnished with fresh sage.

CALZONE

FOR THE BREAD DOUGH:
1½ oz/40 g fresh yeast
pinch of caster sugar
13 oz/375 g plain flour
3 tbsp olive oil
salt and freshly ground black pepper
FOR THE FILLING:
8 oz/225 g ricotta cheese
4 oz/100 g mozzarella cheese, grated
I oz/25 g pitted black olives, sliced
I tbsp freshly chopped oregano
4 oz/100 g sliced Italian salami,
    chopped
2 ripe tomatoes, roughly chopped
2 tbsp tomato purée
fresh oregano to garnish

SERVES 4 • CALORIES PER PORTION: 772

Preheat the oven to Gas 7, 425°F, 220°C, 15 mins before baking. To make the dough, using a fork cream the fresh yeast and sugar together until soft, then stir in 4 tbsp lukewarm water.

Sieve the flour into a bowl, make a well in the centre and add the yeast mixture. Stir in 2 tbsp olive oil, salt and freshly ground black pepper and enough water to form a pliable dough. Knead the dough on a lightly floured surface for 3-4 mins, then cover and leave in a warm place until the dough has doubled in size.

Meanwhile, prepare the filling. Sieve the ricotta cheese into a bowl, then stir in the mozzarella cheese, olives, oregano, salami, tomatoes and tomato purée. Season with salt and freshly ground black pepper, and reserve.

When the dough has doubled in size knead again and divide into four. On a lightly floured surface, flatten each piece into an 8 in/20.5 cm round.

Divide filling into four, then place a portion of filling on one half of each dough round. Moisten edges of the dough with a little water, then fold in half, encasing filling. Seal the edges. Transfer to a greased baking sheet, then, with a sharp knife, cut small slits in top of each. Brush with remaining oil and bake for 30 mins, or until golden.

Garnish with oregano, and served hot with a crisp salad.

MARSALA FIGS

4 ripe figs, wiped
¼ pint/150 ml sweet Marsala wine
4 tbsp mascarpone cheese
2 tbsp ground almonds
4 whole almonds
mint sprigs to decorate

SERVES 4 • CALORIES PER PORTION: 333

Starting at the top of each fig and without cutting all the way through, slice each into quarters to open out the fruit. Place the

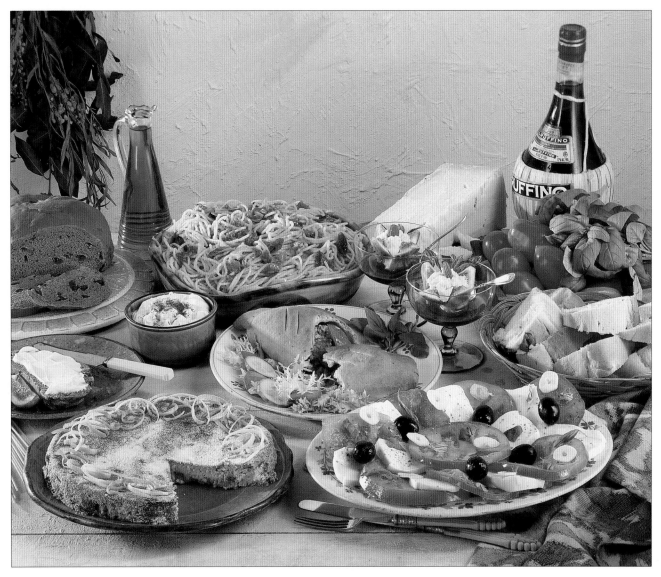

Clockwise from bottom left: rich Ricotta Cheesecake; Spaghetti Alla Carbonara; Marsala Figs; Tomato & Mozzarella Salad, served with fresh olive bread; and centre, Calzone

figs in a shallow dish and pour the Marsala wine over. Cover and leave for about 1 hr.

Meanwhile, mix together the mascarpone cheese and ground almonds, and leave to chill in the fridge until required.

Remove the figs from the Marsala wine and stand each fig in a serving dish. Spoon some of the Marsala wine over fruit, then place some of the prepared cheese mixture in the centre. Top with an almond and decorate with mint sprigs. Serve immediately.

RICOTTA CHEESECAKE

2 oz/50 g sultanas
2 tbsp rum
12 oz/350 g ricotta cheese
3 egg yolks, size 3, beaten
4 oz/100 g caster sugar
2 oz/50 g ground almonds
2 oz/50 g chopped mixed peel
finely grated rind of I lemon
finely grated rind of I orange
vanilla sugar for dusting
orange and lemon zest to decorate

SERVES 4 • CALORIES PER PORTION: 360

Preheat the oven to Gas 4, 350°F, 180°C, 10 mins before baking. Grease and lightly flour a 7 in/18 cm round cake tin. Mix sultanas and rum, leave for 30 mins.

Meanwhile, sieve the ricotta cheese into a bowl, then beat in the egg yolks and caster sugar. Fold in the almonds, mixed peel, grated rinds and the sultana mixture. Mix well and pour into prepared tin. Bake for 30-40 mins, or until firm and shrunken from the sides of tin.

Turn the oven off, open the door and leave the cheesecake to cool with the oven door ajar.

When cool, carefully remove the cheesecake from the tin. Dust with vanilla sugar and decorate with orange and lemon zest to serve.

For an extra-rich treat, serve the cheesecake with whipped cream.

MEXICAN MEAL

Mexican food mustn't be missed with its delicious spiced turkey, rice salads, tasty beans, nachos and spicy dips. It's quick and easy to prepare and simple to cook. So go on, treat your family and friends to a real mouthful of Mexico!

Clockwise from bottom left: Mexican Meatballs; Chunky Beef & Vegetable Soup; Mexican-Style Rice; Exotic Fruit Cocktail; Burritos; and centre, Mole de Guajolote

CHUNKY BEEF & VEGETABLE SOUP

1½ lb/675 g braising steak, trimmed and cubed

1½ pint/900 ml beef stock

2 bay leaves

8 oz/225 g potatoes, peeled and cubed

2 carrots, peeled and chopped

2 courgettes, trimmed and thickly sliced

2 sticks celery, trimmed and chopped

1 red pepper, deseeded and chopped

2 onions, peeled and quartered

SERVES 4-6 •CALORIES PER PORTION: 190-290

Place the meat in a large saucepan, cover with the stock and add bay leaves. Bring to the boil. Cover and simmer for 2 hrs or until the meat is tender. Allow the meat to cool. Remove meat, strain the cooking liquid and return both to a clean pan. Bring to the boil, add the potato and carrot and simmer for 20 mins. Add the remaining ingredients and continue to simmer for 15 mins. Serve hot in bowls with rice and salad.

MOLE DE GUAJOLOTE

FOR THE MARINADE:

3 tbsp vinegar

1 garlic clove, peeled and crushed

4 tbsp soy sauce

pinch of cinnamon

salt and freshly ground black pepper

¼ tsp sugar

3 lb/1.5 kg chicken or turkey, cut into portions and skinned

4 tbsp oil

FOR THE SAUCE:

2 oz/50 g sesame seeds

1 oz/25 g ground almonds

2 oz/50 g cashew nuts, chopped

1-3 tbsp hot chilli powder

2 garlic cloves, peeled and crushed

½-1 tsp ground cinnamon

½-1 tsp ground cumin

2 onions, peeled and finely chopped

¼ pint/150 ml chicken stock

3 tbsp tomato ketchup

¼ pint/150 ml carton soured cream

SERVES 4 • CALORIES PER PORTION: 800

Mix the vinegar, garlic, soy sauce, cinnamon, salt, pepper and sugar together, pour over the chicken or turkey, then cover and chill overnight.

Remove the meat from the marinade and drain, reserving the marinade. Fry the meat in the oil until browned. Drain thoroughly then place in a large saucepan. Pour the reserved marinade over, add 1¼ pints/750 ml water, bring to the boil, cover and simmer, stirring occasionally until the meat is well cooked. Allow to cool and then discard all the bones. Reserve cooking liquid.

Grill the sesame seeds, almonds and cashews for a few minutes until brown. Place them with the chilli powder, garlic, spices, onions and stock in a food processor, blend until smooth. Gradually stir in the ketchup, then the meat with the reserved cooking liquid. Simmer gently until sauce is thick and creamy. Stir continuously, gradually add soured cream and gently heat through. Serve with rice or tortillas and yogurt if liked.

MEATBALLS IN SPICY SAUCE

2 onions, peeled and chopped

8 oz/225 g minced beef

8 oz/225 g minced pork

1 garlic clove, peeled and finely chopped

2 tsp freshly chopped oregano

1 egg, size 3, beaten

salt and freshly ground black pepper

2 tbsp oil

9.52 oz/270 g jar taco sauce

14 oz/397 g can chopped tomatoes

1 green pepper, deseeded and chopped

1 red pepper, deseeded and chopped

SERVES 4-6 • CALORIES PER PORTION: 200-300

Preheat the oven to Gas 6, 400°F, 200°C. Place half the onion, the minced beef, pork, garlic, oregano and beaten egg in a large bowl, and mix thoroughly. Season well.

MEXICAN-STYLE RICE

8 oz/225 g long-grain rice
½ tsp salt
I tbsp oil
I onion, peeled and chopped
I garlic clove, peeled and crushed
14 oz/397 g can tomatoes
12 oz/340 g can sweetcorn, drained
I red pepper, deseeded and roughly
   chopped
I green pepper, deseeded and
   roughly chopped
salt and freshly ground black pepper
I tbsp freshly chopped coriander
2 tbsp unsalted cashew nuts, toasted

SERVES 4 • CALORIES PER PORTION: 325

Cook rice in a pan of boiling salted water for 12-15 mins, or until tender. Meanwhile, heat the oil and cook the onion and garlic until soft. Add the tomatoes, sweetcorn and peppers and simmer gently for 5-10 mins. Drain rice and add to the tomato mixture. Season. Mix well and add the chopped coriander and cashew nuts. Serve either hot or cold.

EXOTIC FRUIT COCKTAIL

I medium pineapple
I pomegranate
I mango, peeled, stoned and sliced
I guava, peeled, stoned and sliced
I banana, peeled and sliced
I orange, peeled and segmented
I red apple, cored and sliced
I tbsp tequila
I tbsp icing sugar

SERVES 4 • CALORIES PER PORTION: 185

Slit the pineapple in half lengthways, carefully cutting through the plume. Scoop out flesh, leaving the shells intact. Discard core, and cut flesh into cubes and place in a bowl. Reserve shells. Remove the fleshy seeds from the pomegranate and add to the bowl. Add the remaining fruits and mix well. Pour the tequila over and add sugar to taste. Then pile the fruit back into pineapple shells or four bowls and serve.

Knead with floured hands until all the mixture holds together, then form the meat into about 20 small balls. Heat the oil in a frying pan and fry the remaining onion until soft. Add meatballs and fry until browned. Remove from the pan and place in an ovenproof casserole. Add the taco sauce, tomatoes and chopped peppers to the pan and simmer gently for 10 mins or until the peppers are soft, then pour over the meatballs. Bake for about 45 mins or until cooked.

BURRITOS

FOR THE TORTILLAS:
8 oz/225 g plain flour
2 level tsp salt
I½ oz/40 g lard, cut into small cubes
FOR THE FRIJOLES (BEANS):
4 tbsp oil
2 onions, peeled and chopped
I garlic clove, peeled and crushed
2 x 15.2 oz/432 g cans chilli beans,
   drained
2 tsp sugar
2 green chillis, deseeded and chopped
   into 4 pieces
I tsp salt

SERVES 8 • CALORIES PER PORTION: 325

To make the tortillas, heat a large non-stick frying pan over a moderate heat and sieve the flour and salt into it. Quickly rub in the fat with the fingertips and gradually stir in approximately 5 fl oz/125 ml warm water until a soft dough is formed. Remove the pan from the heat and knead the dough gently on a floured board. While keeping the rest of the dough covered with damp greaseproof paper, take a small ball of the dough, flatten it and roll out very thinly. Then cut a 9 in/23 cm circle of pastry and add the trimmings to the remaining dough. Continue this process until all the dough is used up. Cook the tortillas in a non-stick frying pan for about 30 seconds each side, remove from the pan and keep warm and covered. For the filling, heat the oil in a large pan and cook the onion until soft. Add the garlic and cook for a further minute or two. Add the beans, sugar, chillis and salt and simmer with ¼ pint/150 ml water for 15 mins. Remove the chillis then drain and mash until a pulp is formed. Add 2 fl oz/50 ml water. Mix well and use as a filling for the tortillas. Serve warm. (In Mexico, beans are served at each meal and refried each time, hence they are known as frijoles refritos, refried beans.)

ORIENTAL FEAST

For a truly delicious taste of the Orient, try these fabulous ideas for cooking in a wok. These simple recipes are certain to be an instant success with the whole family!

CHICKEN & HAM SOUP

FOR THE CROUTONS:
2 slices white bread
4 tbsp vegetable oil
FOR THE SOUP:
1½ pint/900 ml fresh chicken stock
3 tbsp dry sherry
1 tbsp dark soy sauce
1 tbsp light soy sauce
pinch of ground coriander
freshly ground black pepper
6 oz/175 g cooked chicken, skinned and diced
4 oz/100 g cooked ham, diced
4 spring onions, trimmed and sliced

SERVES 4 • CALORIES PER PORTION: 260

To make the croûtons, discard the crusts from the bread and cut bread into small cubes. Heat oil in a wok until just smoking, then fry bread cubes for 2-3 mins, or until golden. Drain on kitchen paper and keep warm until required.

Clean and dry the wok ready to make the soup. Add the chicken stock, sherry, soy sauces and coriander to the wok, then season with the freshly ground black pepper. Bring to the boil, add the diced cooked chicken and ham, then simmer for 10 mins, or until the soup is thoroughly heated through.

To serve, place spring onions in the base of four soup bowls, then pour the soup over the top.

Serve immediately with the freshly cooked croûtons.

SPICED DEEP-FRIED PRAWNS

20 cooked Dublin Bay prawns
1 tsp ground coriander
1 tsp ground cumin
1 garlic clove, peeled and crushed
2 tbsp soy sauce
2 tbsp vegetable oil
FOR THE BATTER:
2 oz/50 g plain flour
1 egg, size 3, beaten
salt and freshly ground black pepper
oil for deep-frying
coriander to garnish

SERVES 4 • CALORIES PER PORTION: 303

Discard the head and shells from the prawns, leaving the tails attached. Using a

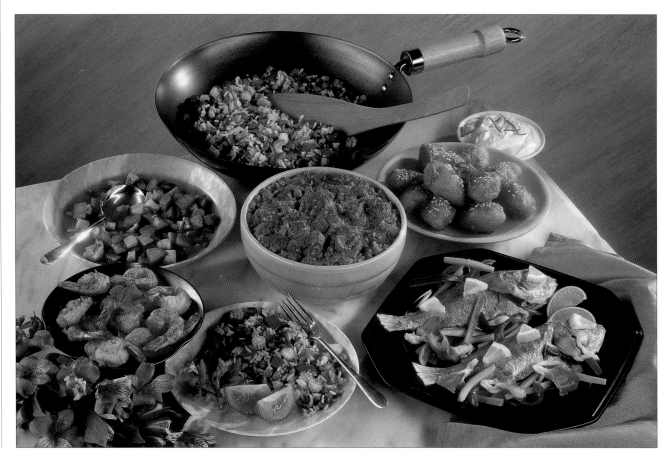

small, sharp knife, carefully slice down the back of each prawn to remove the vein. Place prawns in a shallow dish and sprinkle with the coriander, cumin, garlic, soy sauce and vegetable oil. Mix well, cover and leave to marinate in fridge for 1 hr.

Meanwhile make the batter. Place flour in a bowl and gradually blend in beaten egg and 4 tbsp water to form a smooth batter. Season and leave until required.

In a wok, heat the oil for deep-frying to 325°F, 160°C. Drain the prawns from the marinade, and discard marinade. Dip prawns into batter, then fry in batches of 5 for 1-2 mins, or until golden and crisp. Garnish with coriander to serve.

BEEF & PEANUT CASSEROLE

2 tbsp vegetable oil
1½ lb/675 g braising steak, trimmed
    and cut into 1 in/2.5 cm cubes
1 onion, peeled and chopped
½ pint/300 ml beef stock
4 oz/100 g unsalted peanuts, finely
    chopped
2 tomatoes, skinned and chopped
1 tsp chilli powder
1 tsp turmeric
salt and freshly ground black pepper
red chilli slices to garnish

SERVES 4 • CALORIES PER PORTION: 449

Heat oil in a wok until just smoking, then stir-fry steak and onion for 5 mins, or until meat is brown and sealed. Add stock, peanuts, tomatoes, chilli powder and turmeric, season and mix well. Bring to boil, reduce to a simmer, then cover with lid or foil and cook for 50 mins, or until steak is just tender. Remove the cover, then simmer, stirring occasionally, for 10 mins, or until sauce has reduced and thickened. Garnish and serve immediately.

Clockwise from bottom left: Spiced Deep-fried Prawns; Chicken & Ham Soup; Vegetable Rice Stir-Fry; Fudgy Bananas; Steamed Fish; and centre, Beef & Peanut Casserole

VEGETABLE RICE STIR-FRY

2 tbsp vegetable oil
2 garlic cloves, peeled and crushed
1 bunch of spring onions, trimmed
    and chopped
1 red pepper, deseeded and chopped
4 oz/100 g baby corn, sliced
4 oz/100 g peas, fresh or frozen
15 oz/435 g can black-eyed beans,
    drained
8 oz/225 g long-grain rice, cooked
1 tbsp sesame oil
1 tsp five-spice powder
salt and freshly ground black pepper
fresh parsley to garnish

SERVES 4 • CALORIES PER PORTION: 365

Heat vegetable oil in a wok until just smoking, then add the garlic, spring onions and red pepper. Stir fry for 1 min, then add the baby corn, peas, beans and rice, and stir-fry for 3-4 mins. Stir in sesame oil and five-spice powder, season to taste, then stir-fry for 2-3 mins. Garnish with parsley to serve.

STEAMED FISH WITH VEGETABLES

FOR THE VEGETABLES:
1 large carrot, peeled and sliced into
    thin strips
1 large courgette, trimmed and
    sliced into thin strips
1 small red onion, peeled and sliced
4 oz/100 g small oyster mushrooms,
    wiped
juice of 1 lemon
juice and finely grated rind of 1 lime
4 tbsp dry white wine
2 tsp clear honey
FOR THE FISH:
4 red snapper or red mullet, each
    weighing about 6 oz/175 g
2 garlic cloves, peeled and thinly
    sliced
salt and freshly ground black pepper
lemon and lime pieces to garnish

SERVES 4 • CALORIES PER PORTION: 155

Place vegetables in a shallow dish. Mix

together lemon and lime juice, lime rind, wine and honey. Pour over vegetables, cover and leave to marinate in the fridge for 1-2 hrs.

Place steaming rack in wok, then pour in enough water to cover the base of the wok. (If you don't have a wok you can use a steamer instead.) Clean and wash the fish. Place garlic in cavities, then season and place on steaming rack. Bring water to boil, cover with lid or foil and steam for 5 mins. Turn fish over, then add marinated vegetables. Spoon marinade over the top, then steam for 10-15 mins, or until fish is tender and the vegetables are just cooked. Garnish to serve.

FUDGY BANANAS

3 oz/75 g self-raising flour
1 egg, size 3, beaten
1 tbsp corn oil
4 large bananas
juice of 1 small lemon
oil for deep-frying
6 oz/175 g light soft brown sugar
4 tsp sesame seeds
mint sprig to decorate

SERVES 4 • CALORIES PER PORTION: 525

Sieve the flour into a small bowl, then beat in the egg and 3½ fl oz/100 ml water to form a smooth batter. Leave to stand for 15 mins, then blend in the corn oil.

Meanwhile, peel and slice each banana into six pieces, then sprinkle with the lemon juice to prevent discoloration. In a wok, heat the oil for deep-frying to 350°F, 180°C. Dip the banana pieces in the batter and fry in batches of six for 2-3 mins, or until lightly golden. Drain well on kitchen paper.

To make the fudge, place the sugar and 4 tbsp water in a pan and heat gently for 1-2 mins, or until the sugar dissolves. Increase the heat and allow the mixture to boil for 1-2 mins.

Coat fried banana pieces in the fudge mixture and place on a wire rack. Sprinkle each with sesame seeds, then transfer to a serving plate. Decorate and serve immediately with crème fraîche topped with lemon and lime zest.

THANKSGIVING DINNER

From the heart of America's East coast try some good old-fashioned mouthwaterers, like Thanksgiving Turkey, Griddle Cakes, Shoo-fly Pie and a lot more!

CLAM CHOWDER

18 fresh hard-shelled clams
4 oz/100 g streaky bacon, derinded and chopped
1 onion, chopped
3 medium-sized potatoes, peeled and diced
salt and freshly ground black pepper
1 pint/600 ml milk
¼ pint/150 ml double cream
fresh parsley sprig to garnish

SERVES 6 • CALORIES PER PORTION: 287

Discard any clams that are open. Scrub remaining clams under cold water, then place in a pan of boiling water. Boil for 5-10 mins until shells open. Drain, reserving any liquid, discarding any clams that are still closed. Take clam flesh out of shells and chop. Dry-fry bacon, drain. Sauté onion in bacon fat until soft. Add potatoes, season. Cook for 10 mins. Stir in clams and reserved liquid, cover and cook for 20 mins. Add three-quarters of bacon, milk and cream. Warm through, adjust seasoning. Top with parsley and remaining bacon, serve.

CANDIED SWEET POTATOES

2 lb/900 g sweet potatoes, washed
4 oz/100 g brown sugar
2 oz/50 g butter

SERVRES 10 • CALORIES PER PORTION: 170

Preheat the oven to Gas 4, 350°F, 180°C, 10 mins before baking potatoes. Boil potatoes in skins for 20 mins. Cool, then peel and slice thickly. Place in small roasting pan. Heat the sugar, 4 tbsp water and butter until well mixed. Pour over potatoes and bake for 30 mins, basting frequently with syrup.

TURKEY WITH RELISH

2 oz/50 g butter or margarine
1 onion, chopped
1 stick celery, chopped
4 oz/100 g shelled pecans, chopped
6 oz/175 g fresh breadcrumbs
2 tbsp freshly chopped parsley
salt and freshly ground black pepper
1 egg yolk, size 3
8 lb/3.5 kg oven-ready turkey, giblets removed
2 tsp corn oil
watercress, cocktail baby corn and red pepper, sliced into rings to garnish
FOR THE CRANBERRY RELISH:
8 oz/225 g cranberries, washed, or thawed if frozen
1 small orange, scrubbed, halved and pips removed
½ lemon, scrubbed, pips removed
½ lime, scrubbed, pips removed
4 tbsp caster sugar

SERVES 10 • CALORIES PER PORTION: 507

Preheat the oven to Gas 4, 350°F, 180°C. Melt fat and sauté onion and celery for 2-3 mins. Remove from heat, then add pecans, breadcrumbs and parsley. Season. Bind together with egg yolk. Use stuffing to fill neck cavity of turkey, then fold neck skin over and secure with a cocktail stick. Truss turkey, if necessary, place in a roasting pan, brush with oil. Roast, uncovered, for 3½-4 hrs, basting occasionally, until thoroughly cooked – when the thigh of the bird is pierced the juices should run clear.

Meanwhile, make the relish. Blend cranberries, orange, lemon and lime halves in a food processor until coarsely chopped, stir in sugar to taste, then chill.

Garnish turkey with watercress, and corn inserted into pepper rings.

BOSTON BAKED BEANS

1 lb/450 g dried haricot beans
1 tsp salt
3 tbsp light soft brown sugar
3 tbsp molasses sugar
1 tbsp dry mustard
2 tbsp tomato ketchup
6 oz/175 g piece of gammon
1 onion, peeled
parsley to garnish

SERVES 4 • CALORIES PER PORTION: 436

Preheat the oven to Gas 4, 350°F, 180°C. Rinse beans and place in a large saucepan with salt and 3 pint/1.7 litres water. Cover, bring to the boil and cook for 10 mins. Leave to stand, covered, for 1 hr.

Mix the sugars, mustard and ketchup. Drain beans, reserving liquid. Place beans in a 4 pint/2.25 litre casserole, stir in sugar mixture. Pour reserved liquid over beans to cover (add water if necessary), stir. Place gammon and onion in centre of beans, cover and bake for 1 hr. Reduce heat to Gas 1, 275°F, 140°C. Bake for 6 hrs. Stir occasionally and top up with water. Remove lid for last 30 mins. Garnish and serve.

GRIDDLE CAKES

8 oz/225 g plain flour
¼ tsp salt
2 tsp baking powder
1 egg, size 3
½ pint/300 ml milk
1 tbsp butter or margarine, melted

SERVES 8 • CALORIES PER PORTION: 147

Sift flour, salt and baking power into bowl. Beat in egg, milk and fat until smooth. Lightly oil a griddle or heavy-based frying pan, heat for 1 min. Cook several pancakes on griddle at once, using 2 tbsp of batter for each. Cook until surfaces of pancakes bubble. Turn and cook until lightly brown on underside. Repeat with remaining batter. Serve warm with melted butter and maple syrup.

BOSTON BROWN BREAD

8 oz/225 g wholemeal flour
4 oz/100 g cornmeal/maizemeal
4 oz/100 g rye flour
1 tsp salt
1 tsp bicarbonate of soda
¼ pint/150 ml black treacle
½ pint/300 ml buttermilk
3 oz/75 g raisins

MAKES 4 LOAVES/8 SLICES EACH
CALORIES PER SLICE: 55

Remove labels from four empty 1 lb/450 g rust-free food cans. Sterilize the cans, dry and grease lightly.

Sieve wholemeal flour, cornmeal or maizemeal, rye flour, salt and bicarbonate of soda into a large bowl. Stir in treacle and buttermilk to form a smooth batter. Fold in raisins. Half fill cans with batter and cover open end with greaseproof paper. Place in pan with enough water to come halfway up sides of tins. Cover pan, bring to boil, simmer for 2-2½ hrs. Turn out bread and serve warm with butter.

SHOO-FLY PIE

6 oz/175 g shortcrust pastry
4 oz/100 g plain flour
½ tsp ground cinnamon
¼ tsp ground ginger
¼ tsp grated nutmeg
2 oz/50 g butter or margarine
2 oz/50 g soft brown sugar
6 tbsp black treacle
1 egg, size 3, lightly beaten
½ tsp baking powder
¼ pint/150 ml whipping cream
crystallized ginger to decorate

SERVES 8 • CALORIES PER PORTION: 333

Preheat the oven to Gas 7, 425°F, 220°C.

Roll out pastry to fit an 8 in/20.5 cm flan ring. Chill. Sieve flour and spices into a bowl. Rub in fat to resemble fine breadcrumbs. Stir in sugar.

Blend treacle with 4 fl oz/120 ml boiling water. Mix together egg and baking powder, then beat in treacle. Pour into pastry case. Top with flour mixture and bake for 10 mins. Reduce oven temperature to Gas 4, 350°F, 180°C. Bake for 30 mins until firm. Cool.

Whip cream until peaking. Spoon evenly around top of pie. Decorate with ginger.

Clockwise from bottom left: delicious Griddle Cakes with maple syrup and butter; Clam Chowder, topped with parsley and bacon; Turkey with Cranberry Relish and Candied Sweet Potatoes; tasty Boston Baked Beans; Boston Brown Bread with butter; and mouthwatering Shoo-fly Pie

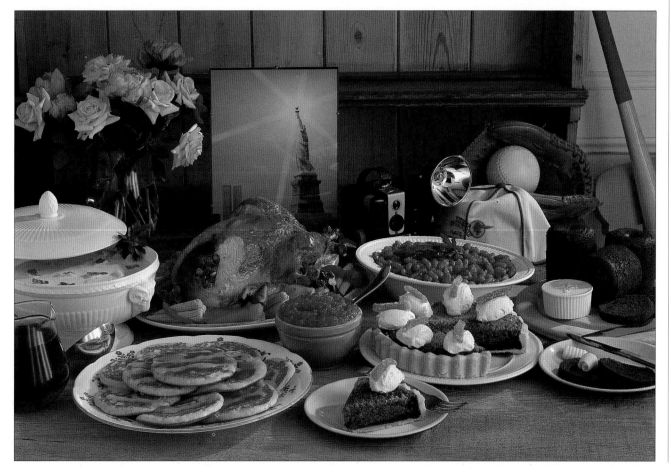

INDEX

ACKNOWLEDGEMENTS

Gina Steer would like to thank the following photographers:
Ian O'Leary
Sue Jorgensen
David Armstrong
Tony Robins

Also many thanks to Jenny Brightman and Kathryn Hawkins for their
assistance in styling and photography.